T0318224

Referees, Match Officials and Abuse

This book explores issues related to the abuse of referees and match officials in sport. Drawing on original empirical research in football, rugby union, rugby league and cricket, it provides an insight into the complexities involved in the recruitment, retention and development processes of match officials from across the global sports industry.

Using an evidence-based approach, the book examines why abuse occurs, the operational environments in which match officials operate, and underlying issues and trends that cut across sports and therefore can be linked to wider societal trends. It challenges global sport policy and discusses the development of an inclusive, cohesive and facilitative environment for match officials, players, coaches and spectators to ensure the future provision of global sport.

Referees, Match Officials and Abuse is an invaluable resource for all students, scholars and national governing bodies of sport with an interest in match officials, sports governance, sport policy, sport management and the sociology of sport.

Tom Webb is Course Leader for the MSc Sports Management and Senior Lecturer in Sports Management and Development at the University of Portsmouth, UK. He is also founder and coordinator of the Referee and Match Official Research Network.

Mike Rayner is Associate Head (Education) at the University of Portsmouth, UK. Mike is a Fellow of The Institute of Leadership and Management (ILM), Fellow of the Chartered Institute for Sports Management and Physical Activity (CIMSPA), a Senior Fellow of the Higher Education Academy and an Academic Member of the Chartered Institute of Personnel and Development (CIPD).

Jamie Cleland is Senior Lecturer in Sport and Management at the University of South Australia. His research explores a range of social issues in sport.

Jimmy O'Gorman is Senior Lecturer in Sports Development, Management and Coaching in the Department of Sport and Physical Activity at Edge Hill University, UK.

Routledge Focus on Sport, Culture and Society

Routledge Focus on Sport, Culture and Society showcases the latest cutting-edge research in the sociology of sport and exercise. Concise in form (20,000–50,000 words) and published quickly (within three months), the books in this series represents an important channel through which authors can disseminate their research swiftly and make an impact on current debates. We welcome submissions on any topic within the socio-cultural study of sport and exercise, including but not limited to subjects such as gender, race, sexuality, disability, politics, the media, social theory, Olympic Studies, and the ethics and philosophy of sport. The series aims to be theoretically-informed, empirically-grounded and international in reach, and will include a diversity of methodological approaches.

List of titles

For more information about this series, please visit: www.routledge.com/sport/series/RFSCS

Referees, Match Officials and Abuse

Research and Implications for Policy

Tom Webb, Mike Rayner, Jamie Cleland and Jimmy O'Gorman

LONDON AND NEW YORK

First published 2021
by Routledge
2 Park Square, Milton Park, Abingdon, Oxon OX14 4RN

and by Routledge
605 Third Avenue, New York, NY 10017

First issued in paperback 2022

Routledge is an imprint of the Taylor & Francis Group, an informa business

Publisher's Note
The publisher has gone to great lengths to ensure the quality of this
reprint but points out that some imperfections in the original copies may
be apparent.

British Library Cataloguing-in-Publication Data
A catalogue record for this book is available from the British Library

Library of Congress Cataloging-in-Publication Data
Names: Webb, Tom (Thomas), author. | Rayner, Mike, 1983– author. |
    Cleland, Jamie, author. | O'Gorman, Jimmy, author.
Title: Referees, match officials and abuse : research and implications
    for policy / Tom Webb, Mike Rayner, Jamie Cleland, Jimmy
    O'Gorman.
Description: Abingdon, Oxon ; New York : Routledge, 2021. |
    Series: Routledge focus on sport, culture and society | Includes
    bibliographical references and index.
Identifiers: LCCN 2020027251 (print) | LCCN 2020027252 (ebook) |
    ISBN 9781138364677 (hardback) | ISBN 9780429431203 (ebook)
Subjects: LCSH: Sports officiating—Psychological aspects. | Sports
    and state. | Violence in sports.
Classification: LCC GV735 .W43 2021 (print) | LCC GV735 (ebook) |
    DDC 796.01/9—dc23
LC record available at https://lccn.loc.gov/2020027251
LC ebook record available at https://lccn.loc.gov/2020027252

ISBN: 978-0-367-63359-2 (pbk)
ISBN: 978-1-138-36467-7 (hbk)
ISBN: 978-0-429-43120-3 (ebk)

DOI: 10.4324/9780429431203

Typeset in Times New Roman
by Apex CoVantage, LLC

Contents

Figures

Tables

Preface

Why are sports match officials verbally and physically abused? How does this abuse occur, in what settings? How long has this abuse been evident and what can, and is, being done about it?

These questions, alongside a myriad of others, drove the conception and formation of this book. Having been involved with research related to sports match officials for over 15 years, and working and writing this book for over two years, as researchers we were interested in whether ongoing media coverage of the issues, governing body attention and not to mention academic research have shifted the agenda and debate. We wanted to give a platform to match officials to explain and detail their experiences of abuse, support networks and the challenges that they encounter when performing their role. In writing this book we have been moved by the accounts and information provided by over 8,000 match officials. The honesty with which they have responded to the online surveys has been refreshing and at times challenging to read and analyse but has ultimately provided a detailed view of the world of the sports match official.

This book offers a comprehensive analysis of the abuse of sports match officials, and therefore provides a considerable resource for match officials, governing bodies and individuals involved in the management and training of match officials across sports and countries. The book utilises empirical research involving match officials in football (soccer), cricket, rugby union and rugby league in England as well as match officials operating in football in France and the Netherlands. Furthermore, we have considered the situation and accounts from sports in other countries through media reports and through governing body policy responses, aimed at tackling the issues related to the abuse of match officials.

This coverage of sports and countries by the conclusion of this book permits a considered and detailed examination of former and current policy interventions, and we present a 10-point plan for any individual involved in the governance of sport and/or sport match officials to consider how they might positively react to any issues related to abuse in their sport. It is important to acknowledge that despite the issues examined in this book, there are stories of positivity, of governing bodies supporting match officials and changing policy to reflect this support. We hope that this book can provide an opportunity for governing bodies to extend this support of match officials further, in different sports and countries around the world.

Therefore, this book and the research that we have conducted are designed to assist in the development of any sport and the match officials therein. This book provides analysis and findings enabling sports to work towards a more inclusive, cohesive and facilitative environment for match officials, players, coaches and spectators, moving towards more sustainable recruitment and retention of match officials. An aim and sentiment that all governing bodies should embrace. Ultimately, if this book can contribute towards a safer environment, enhanced match official support and development systems, a more content match official workforce and a roadmap for future governing body policy interventions and initiatives then the construction and time spent on this book will have been worthwhile.

Tom Webb, PhD,
University of Portsmouth, UK

Acknowledgements

The authors would like to thank all of the referees, umpires and match officials who have taken the time to contribute to this research. Without your input the book could not have been as comprehensive as you have helped to make it. We would like to thank any governing bodies who have contributed to the research and we would also like to acknowledge the UEFA Research Grant Programme who funded some of the research involved in the production of this book.

1 Introducing and defining match official abuse

Scope of the book

The purpose of this book is to bring together a burgeoning body of research that has explored a) the propensity of abuse experienced by sports officials,[1] b) the impact of abuse directed towards sports officials, and c) the efficacy of policy and strategic responses devised to combat abuse towards sports officials. The scope of this body of research centres on the abuse of sports officials operating at mass participation levels through to professional levels in England across the sports of football, cricket rugby union and rugby league, and is supplemented by research examining the abuse directed towards football referees in France and the Netherlands. Therefore, this book focuses on modern sports officials operating in the 21st century and the challenges associated with their roles.

Abuse directed towards sports match officials is not a recent phenomenon. Forms of abuse have existed since before codification in some sports in England. However, despite the longevity of this abuse towards match officials, there are few indicators that this abuse is declining. In fact, there is evidence to suggest that abuse towards match officials across different sports is increasing, rather than decreasing in both frequency and severity (Webb, Rayner, & Thelwell, 2019). As a result of this prolonged abuse, this issue has drawn academic attention, particularly over the past 10–15 years (Cleland, O'Gorman, & Bond, 2015; Cleland, O'Gorman, & Webb, 2018; Dell, Gervis, & Rhind, 2016; Kellett & Shilbury, 2007; Rayner, Webb, & Webb, 2016; Warner, Tingle, & Kellett, 2013).

There are interrelated areas of research which have focused upon the formal and informal support networks around match officials (Kellett & Warner, 2011; Webb, Dicks, Thelwell, van der Kamp, & Rix-Lievre, 2020), with links between discontinuation and a perceived lack of support identified (Ridinger, Kim, Warner, & Tingle, 2017a; Ridinger, Warner, Tingle, & Kim, 2017b). The issues concerning abuse and support can also be associated to those matters which have been discovered in football in England (Cleland et al., 2018; Webb, Cleland, & O'Gorman, 2017), as well as rugby union (Rayner et al., 2016), cricket (Webb et al., 2019) and rugby league (Webb, Rayner, & Thelwell, 2018).

This book primarily draws upon a number of empirical studies using survey research methods which have explored the abuse of sports officials, the support provided to them, their training to deal with abuse, and their experiences of policy and strategy responses to abuse. In sum, the voices of 8,010 officials ranging from elite professional through to mass participation amateur sport in football, cricket, rugby union and rugby league have been captured through online surveys (6,693 football referees, with 2,056 from England, 3,408 from France and 1,229 from the Netherlands; 456 rugby union referees; 89 rugby league referees; and 772 cricket umpires). The data collected were both quantitative and qualitative, with the online surveys designed to capture numeric representations of a large-scale population of sports officials and, through open questions, providing them with the opportunity to comment on their experiences.

All the online surveys had the collective objectives of considering match official abuse, support and training. In order for the illustrative quotations that are utilised throughout the book to be clear and applied most effectively, the sport, sex, length of time officiating and age group of the match official in question are noted. It is the intention of this book to unpack the issues surrounding the abuse of sports match officials, as well as factors which can contribute to abuse and impact upon abuse, and the implications of this research for policy makers and those in governance roles at national and international sports governing bodies.

History of sport official abuse

The propensity for sports officials to routinely suffer both verbal and physical abuse can largely be traced back to the codification processes of modern sport forms in England spanning the 18th and 19th centuries (Webb, 2017), although this often depended on the sport in question. For example, after the codification of association football (hereafter football) in 1863 the game grew and resulted in professionalism being accepted in 1885 by the Football Association (the game's governing body) at a time when leagues were being formed (Cleland, 2015).

Over time, the onus on winning and implications of poor results increased the pressure on players, coaches and consequently referees. As such, the professionalisation of the sport in the latter part of the 18th century was frequently accompanied by abuse aimed towards the official. This was often initiated by crowds through the unwanted attention of abusive gamblers who felt that refereeing decisions had negatively affected their team's performance, and consequently their wager (Webb, 2016). It was not uncommon for football referees to receive threats from crowds and following the match itself abusive and threatening letters to their home address (Webb, 2016, 2017). The aggressive behaviour of spectators or supporters was a particular concern to authorities, and ground closures were a common occurrence from 1895–1915 (Dunning, Murphy, & Williams, 1988; Lewis, 1906).

Cricket had similar concerns to football. Even after the foundation of the Marylebone Cricket Club (MCC) in 1787 leading to codification, umpires, who were utilised as a third party to settle disputes (Malcolm, 2001), were also the subject of unwanted attention related to the behaviour of gamblers during and after the fixtures (Malcolm, 1999). These issues were also evident amongst cricket crowds in the stadiums, with a number of stadia built or purchased at the start of the 20th century (Vamplew, 1980).

Cricket has much of its historical grounding in England and is not alone in that respect. For example, rugby union also has similar foundations and, furthermore, both sports exhibit an inherent acceptance of sportsmanship, rules and the authority and decision making of the match official (Dunning & Sheard, 2005). Rugby union was codified in 1871 and has retained a fairly constant structure as the game has evolved (Collins, 2009). However, there is also historical evidence of abuse directed towards officials in rugby during the bifurcation of the rules and subsequent codification of two versions of the sport which was largely based upon distinctions of social class (Collins, 2012).

In the late 1870s the organisation of cup competitions in rugby league led to disorderly crowd behaviour, with attention being placed on the referee's decisions (Collins, 2012). Incidents arose due to the partisan nature of the supporter relationships between working class towns in the north of the UK. For example, the Wakefield Trinity team was attacked by Halifax supporters after their 1879 final victory in revenge for Trinity's semi-final defeat of Halifax. Moreover, a referee named Harry Garnett was escorted from various grounds by the police following Yorkshire Cup ties after supporters disputed some of his decisions and wanted to accost him personally (Collins, 2012).

An example reported by the *Yorkshire Post* newspaper in 1893 suggested that aggression towards match officials in a rugby union fixture was expressed in particular by working-class players and spectators because they jeered and heckled referees as well as the opposing team. This was also the case with those subject to British imperial rule overseas, with referee decisions often questioned and subjected to shouting and whistling (Collins, 1998). Furthermore, the Paris Olympics in 1924 produced unwanted attention for the rugby union referee involved. An unexpected defeat for France to a team from the USA (essentially made up of players from Stanford, some of whom had also won the previous tournament in 1920), led to the referee requiring police protection following unrest amongst the crowd (Richards, 2006).

These historical examples serve to remind us that since the advent of routinised, regular, codified competitive sport, the abuse of officials as independent arbiters of the rules has been common, and largely uncritically accepted as 'part of the game' (Vamplew, 1980). We can still see evidence of this negative behaviour today, although player and match official behaviour is evolving as technology has been introduced into the professional game (Webb & Rayner, 2016), with the changes in finance and media exposure exacerbated by the technological developments (Armenteros & Webb, 2019; Webb, 2018). This development of technology and heightened exposure has also increased the routine analysis of the decision making and performance of sports match officials, particularly given the high stakes involved in the elite professional leagues (Webb, 2018).

These issues are not confined to one sport, such as football, or even to a specific country, such as England. Therefore, this book initially considers the situation in England before widening the focus to countries outside the UK in later chapters, focusing on the extent of the abuse experience by sports officials, any impact of this abuse and the policy implications for governing bodies of sport. Furthermore, this book considers modern sports officials operating in sports in the 21st century and the challenges associated with their roles. As such, it is important to understand the current challenges that are being faced in terms of match official abuse, with high-profile incidents often keeping this subject in the public eye.

The current situation

We have seen high-profile organisations such as the Fédération Internationale de Football Association (FIFA) warning national football associations, as well as players, coaches and spectators, that there will be a global shortage of referees, should the trend of abuse towards them continue (Swanson, 2018). High-profile incidents also increase the exposure and tension around the issue of match official abuse. Three high-profile incidents in different sports are identified and explained in the following section in order to give further context to the issues which match officials in elite sports face and the exposure that some of these incidents receive in the media:

1 In football, the Juventus goalkeeper Gianluigi Buffon was sent off by referee Michael Oliver in a Champions League quarter final match

between Juventus and Real Madrid in 2018, following the award of a penalty towards the end of the game. Buffon reacted angrily to the decision on the pitch, confronting the referee. Buffon also spoke after the match, describing the referee as an "animal" and also claiming that he had "a rubbish bin instead of a heart" (de Menezes, 2018). The reaction of the player, the subsequent post-match comments and the final result (Juventus were eliminated from the competition by Real Madrid after they scored the penalty which Buffon originally protested about) meant further abuse directed towards the referee and his family from Juventus supporters. These actions were strongly condemned by the Union of European Football Associations (UEFA) (Conn, 2018).

2   In rugby union, the Sale Sharks director of rugby, Steve Diamond, was given a six-week stadium ban in 2017 for comments made about the referee following Sale's defeat by Exeter. Diamond accused the referee of "making it up" and compared the standard of officiating in England to European rugby, commenting, "We found out in Europe the refereeing is abysmal, and we found out tonight [against Exeter] that if referees want to come up here and make it up, then they can do" (BBC Sport, 2017). Incidents such as this forced the Rugby Football Union (RFU) and Premiership Rugby to attempt the enforcement of a "crack down" on this type of behaviour (Jones, 2018).

3   In cricket, red cards have been introduced globally in a move by the Marylebone Cricket Club (MCC), the governors of the laws of the game of cricket across the world, to reduce and control the abuse directed towards umpires at all levels of the game (Martin, 2016). Red cards have been deemed necessary in cricket due to the growing culture of abuse towards umpires. For example, the Australian bowler Josh Hazlewood was fined 15% of his match fee for dissent after confronting an umpire in a test match against New Zealand in 2016, prompting the International Cricket Committee (ICC) to remark that "the behaviour in some matches by some players was deemed unacceptable and not a good example to young fans" (The Guardian, 2016).

Following these examples, and the exploration of existent research, it is also imperative that we define what we mean by abuse, and how abuse has been covered in the sports-related literature.

Defining abuse

Historically, much of the literature concerning manifestations of abuse in sport has centred on child protection and safeguarding (Brackenridge, 1994, 2004; Brackenridge, Bringer, & Bishop, 2005; Hartill & Lang, 2014), and sexual abuse (Brackenridge, Bishopp, Moussalli, & Tapp, 2008; Dixon, 2019; Fasting, Brackenridge, & Sundgot-Borgen, 2003). Indeed, the emergence of much of the research concerning emotional abuse in sport has built upon understandings of the literature regarding child abuse (Stirling & Kerr, 2013). Whilst we acknowledge that sports officials are bound up in such issues, the types of abuse experienced by them are less likely to be related to child protection issues or sexual abuse. However, research related to the abuse of sports officials is an underexplored area and this book focuses specifically on the abuse to which these sports officials are subjected.

Abuse towards sports match officials is more likely to involve aggression and verbal/physical abuse (Webb et al., 2017). The classification of this abuse is important to comprehend in order to develop understanding of the experiences of match officials across sports, and at varying levels of officiating in sport. We can draw upon the guidelines which the American Professional Society on the Abuse of Children (APSAC) have published (APSAC, 1995) to inform further about the classifications of abuse before linking this to sport specifically.

The APSAC guidelines (1995) describe six specific areas of psychological maltreatment, three of which can be applied to sport and match officials. These are: a) spurning (verbal and non-verbal hostile rejecting/degrading), b) terrorising (behaviour that threatens or is likely to harm physically) and c) isolating (denying opportunities for interacting/communicating with peers or others). The APSAC guidelines are useful to explore the categories of maltreatment, and research has extended this understanding to link these concepts of maltreatment. This is part of the wider area of maltreatment alongside physical and emotional abuse, sexual abuse, harassment/discriminatory abuse, neglect and bullying (Glaser, 2002). Of these areas, we can count emotional abuse as verbal abuse (defined as terrorising verbal abuse), where behaviour threatens harm towards an individual or their family/friends (Glaser, 2002). However, it is how abuse exists in sport which is important here, and in particular how this abuse can be understood when directed towards sports officials.

Abuse can be categorised into relational maltreatment and non-relational maltreatment in sport. For example, Stirling (2009) created a conceptual framework categorising both verbal emotional abuse and contact physical abuse under the wider subsection of relational maltreatment. Emotional abuse can be described as a pattern of deliberate non-contact behaviours within a critical relationship (match officials, players, coaches and spectators for example) that has the potential to be harmful, or have consequences to the individual receiving the emotional abuse, occurring more frequently as emotional abuse becomes more pronounced as their careers progress (Stirling & Kerr, 2008a, 2008b). Individuals involved in sport can experience emotional abuse within the relationships that are formed, although historically research has tended to concentrate on the coach-athlete relationship rather than the match official in sport (Stirling, 2013). Research has identified that abuse within these relationships can include negative physical behaviour, such as throwing objects or punching walls, and negative verbal behaviour, such as ridicule and humiliating remarks (Stirling, 2013).

When considering match officials specifically in this book, we are concerned with two particular aspects of abuse, emotional abuse and physical abuse, and in particular a specific aspect or classification of emotional abuse, termed verbal abuse (Marshall, 2012). Therefore, the terms verbal emotional abuse and contact physical abuse are referred to as verbal and physical abuse throughout this book. These two aspects of abuse occur within the context of a critical relationship, where the relationship between the actors has significant influence over an individual's sense of safety, in a setting such as a sporting fixture (Stirling, 2009). When relating this to match officials, we are concerned with matters which are central to the effective provision of match officials, such as their experiences, safety and motivation to continue in their respective sport.

Violence and aggression have long been an accepted part of sport, and the term aggression itself "includes such wide-ranging acts . . . as physically hitting another individual and verbal abuse" (Tenenbaum, Singer, Stewart, & Duda, 1997, p. 1). Donahue, Rip, and Vallerand (2009) observed that obsessively passionate basketball players were found to associate with aggressive behaviour, whereas the existence of boundaries related to aggressive behaviour in different sports and levels of competition allowed for individual judgements, from people such as match officials (Burton, 2005). Supporters have also been identified as a distinct group who demonstrate both physical and verbal aggression. Indeed, supporter dysfunction related positively to perceptions of the appropriateness of verbal aggression and physical aggression (Donahue & Wann, 2009). Moreover, supporters in highly identified groups reported higher levels of hostile aggression than fans low in identification, with any aggression directed toward the match officials often hostile in nature (Wann, Carlson, & Schrader, 1999).

This leads us back to the notion of abuse towards the match official in sport. We have seen that there are high-profile incidents in a variety of sports at the elite level; however, the wider issue lies at the lower levels of sport, at the mass participation levels, where verbal and physical abuse towards match officials is the most prevalent (Webb et al., 2019). Indeed, match officials have discussed emergent trends at youth and grassroots levels following incidents in professional sport, identifying that there is a link between occurrences and incidents at the top of their respective sports and in the subsequent behaviour of players, coaches and spectators at lower levels (Webb et al., 2019).

Most match officials operate at a mass participation level (for example in English football, in the 2016/2017 season, there were 28,037 referees of which 66.5% were Level 7² or below; Referee Development Day Presentation, 2017) and most match officials are effectively volunteers, people who receive expenses for travel, but do not receive a wage. However, they are also vitally important to the wider structure of sport in England and other countries around the world. Without sports match officials we do not have the structure of sport and physical activity which exists today. In short, match officials can be seen as facilitators of physical activity at many levels of sport.

Structure of the book

The empirical research that underpins this book has, following extensive analysis of the data, facilitated the construction of themes, which can cut across any particular sport. Therefore, the subsequent chapters are organised thematically and represent the key findings from the online surveys completed by over 8,000 sports match officials. Chapter 2 considers the existence and extent of abuse towards match officials, utilising specific examples to illustrate abuse, the settings for abuse and how abuse manifests itself from the perspective of match officials. The chapter also considers the role of governing bodies in dealing with abuse towards match officials and considers how match officials are experiencing diminishing enjoyment due to the prolonged abuse of players, coaches and spectators. A significant concern for those in positions of governance. Chapter 3 identifies the reporting and disciplinary processes, including the reasons behind the non-reporting of abuse by some match officials, the implications of non-reporting and the dysfunctional disciplinary processes for match officials and administrators. It also considers the existence of cultures of abuse across sports, the importance of organisational culture and performance and the influence that these facets can have upon the experiences and performances of match officials. An environment characterised by abuse being both ignored and accepted, a reluctance and lack of effective action from governing bodies and as a result, a workforce who have reservations about continuing in the role are all aspects that are concerning for governing bodies.

Chapter 4 focuses upon the importance of support networks for match officials, given the abuse to which they can be subjected. The support provided to match officials by professional associations such as governing bodies, referee organisations and the leagues in which they officiate, is focused upon, as is the support provided by personal support networks. The role and importance of resilience, particularly important for match officials, is contemplated alongside the prominence of mental fortitude in challenging situations. Moreover, the skills developed by match officials to manage inter-group conflict and resolve conflict are discussed.

Chapter 5 explores match officials' perceptions of policy interventions in their sports and implications for future policy objectives of governing bodies. We focus upon the impact that policy decisions can have on match officials, providing examples of policy interventions and experiences of match officials themselves. Mental health policy and interventions are considered, with the importance of better support around match officials in the current sporting climate considered. The evolving focus on wellbeing and mental health is examined, although further enhancements are identified as an essential part of the requirement to increase support around match officials, something which the introduction of the conceptual model of the factors influencing match official welfare and future outcomes considers further.

Chapter 6 places some of the findings from the previous chapters into context by considering the experiences of match officials outside England. The chapter includes a detailed review of media reports across different sports and countries across the world, to help ascertain the extent of the problem and explain the current situation in which match officials currently exist. Alongside these media reports, research conducted with football referees in France and the Netherlands is analysed to contextualise the experiences of match officials outside England, in order to learn from these trends and ultimately reduce the abuse which exists.

Finally, the concluding chapter, Chapter 7, focuses upon the policy implications of the findings identified across the book and the potential solutions. Areas of good practice are raised in order to initiate conversations across sports and countries as a method of addressing the shared trends identified across the book. Gaps in the research and potential areas for future exploration and development are also explored as a means of developing wider academic interest in this emergent research area.

Notes

1 Throughout this book the terms sports officials, sports match officials, match officials, referees and umpires are used interchangeably.
2 Level 7 is part of the development and progression pathway.

References

APSAC. (1995). *Psychosocial evaluation of suspected psychological maltreatment in children and adolescents: Practice guidelines.* American Professional Society on the Abuse of Children. Retrieved from https://apsac.memberclicks. net/assets/documents/PracticeGuidelines/psychosocial%20evaluation%20of%20 suspected%20psychosocial%20maltreatment.pdf

Armenteros, M., & Webb, T. (2019). Educating international football referees: The importance of uniformity. In M. Armenteros, A. J. Benitez, & M. A. Betancor (Eds.), *The use of video technologies in refereeing football and other sports* (pp. 301–327). London: Routledge.

BBC Sport. (2017). *Steve Diamond: Sale Sharks director of rugby given six-week stadium ban.* Retrieved from www.bbc.co.uk/sport/rugby-union/42025775

Brackenridge, C. H. (1994). Fair play or fair game? Child sexual abuse in sport organisations. *International Review for the Sociology of Sport, 29*(3), 287–298. doi: 10.1177/101269029402900304

Brackenridge, C. H. (2004). Women and children first? Child abuse and child protection in sport. *Sport in Society, 7*(3), 322–337. doi: 10.1080/1743043042000291668

Brackenridge, C. H., Bishopp, D., Moussalli, D., & Tapp, J. (2008). The characteristics of sexual abuse in sport: A multidimensional scaling analysis of events described in media reports. *International Journal of Sport and Exercise Psychology, 6*(4), 385–406. doi: 10.1080/1612197X.2008.9671881

Brackenridge, C. H., Bringer, J. D., & Bishopp, D. (2005). Managing cases of abuse in sport. *Journal of Theoretical Social Psychology, 14*(4), 259–274. doi: 10.1002/car.900

Burton, R. W. (2005). Aggression and sport. *Clinics in Sports Medicine, 24*, 845–852. doi: 10.1016/j.csm.2005.03.001

Cleland, J. (2015). *A sociology of football in a global context.* London: Routledge.

Cleland, J., O'Gorman, J., & Bond, M. (2015). The English football association's respect campaign: The referees' view. *International Journal of Sport, Policy and Politics, 7*(4), 551–563. doi: 10.1080/19406940.2015.1088050

Cleland, J., O'Gorman, J., & Webb, T. (2018). Respect? An investigation into the experience of referees in association football. *International Review for the Sociology of Sport, 53*(8), 960–974. doi: 10.1177/1012690216687979

Collins, T. (1998). Racial minorities in a marginalized sport: Race, discrimination and integration in British rugby league football. *Immigrants & Minorities: Historical Studies in Ethnicity, Migration and Diaspora, 17*(1), 151–169. doi: 10.1080/02619288.1998.9974933

Collins, T. (2009). *A social history of English rugby union.* London: Routledge.

Collins, T. (2012). *Rugby's great split: Class, culture and the origins of rugby league football.* Oxon: Frank Cass.

Conn, D. (2018). Gianluigi Buffon is in the wrong: Referees need respect. *Guardian Website.* Retrieved from www.theguardian.com/football/blog/2018/apr/12/grassroots-referees-fallout-gianluigi-buffon-outburst

Dell, C., Gervis, M., & Rhind, D. (2016). Factors influencing soccer referee's intentions to quit the game. *Soccer & Society, 17*(1), 109–119. doi: 10.1080/14660970.2014.919275

De Menezes, J. (2018). *Gianluigi Buffon apologises to referee Michael Oliver for going "beyond the limits" after Champions League red card.* Retrieved from www.independent.co.uk/sport/football/european/gianluigi-buffon-michael-oliver-referee-apology-juventus-vs-real-madrid-a8355696.html

Dixon, K. (2019). Sexual abuse and masculine cultures: Reflections on the British football scandal of 2016. In R. Magrath, J. Cleland, & E. Anderson (Eds.), *The Palgrave handbook of masculinity and sport* (pp. 73–93). Switzerland: Palgrave Macmillan.

Donahue, E. G., Rip, B., & Vallerand, R. J. (2009). When winning is everything: On passion, identity, and aggression in sport. *Psychology of Sport and Exercise, 10*(5), 526–534. doi: 10.1016/j.psychsport.2009.02.002

Donahue, T., & Wann, D. L. (2009). Perceptions of the appropriateness of sport fan physical and verbal aggression: Potential influences of team identification and fan dysfunction. *North American Journal of Psychology, 11*(3), 419–428.

Dunning, E., Murphy, P. M., & Williams, J. (1988). *The roots of football hooliganism: An historical and sociological study.* London: Routledge & Keegan Paul.

Dunning, E., & Sheard, K. (2005). *Barbarians, gentlemen and players: A sociological study of rugby football.* London: Routledge.

Fasting, K., Brackenridge, C., & Sundgot-Borgen, J. (2003). Experiences of sexual harassment and abuse among Norwegian elite female athletes and nonathletes. *Research Quarterly for Exercise and Sport, 74*(1), 84–97. doi: 10.1080/02701367. 2003.10609067

Glaser, D. (2002). Emotional abuse and neglect (psychological maltreatment): A conceptual framework. *Child Abuse & Neglect, 26*(6–7), 697–714. doi: 10.1016/ S0145-2134(02)00342-3

The Guardian. (2016). Australia's Josh Hazlewood fined after angry confrontation with umpire. Retrieved from www.theguardian.com/sport/2016/feb/23/ josh-hazlewood-facing-sanction-after-angry-confrontation-with-umpire

Hartill, M. & Lang, M. (2014). "I know people think i'm a complete pain in the neck": An examination of the introduction of child protection and "safeguarding" in English sport from the perspective of national governing body safeguarding lead officers. *Social Sciences, 3*(4), 606-627.

Jones, S. (2018). *Rugby refs to players: Stop the abuse and backchat.* Retrieved from www.thetimes.co.uk/article/rugby-refs-to-players-stop-the-abuse-and-back-chat-9m36kc578

Kellett, P., & Shilbury, D. (2007). Umpire participation: Is abuse really the issue? *Sport Management Review, 10*(3), 209–229. doi: 10.1016/S1441-3523(07)70012-8

Kellett, P., & Warner, S. (2011). Creating communities that lead to retention: The social worlds and communities of umpires. *European Sport Management Quarterly, 11*(5), 471–494. doi: 10.1080/16184742.2011.624109

Lewis, J. (1906). The much abused referee. In *The book of football: A complete history and record of the association and rugby games* (pp. 263–264). London: The Amalgamated Press Ltd.

Malcolm, D. (1999). Cricket spectator disorder: Myths and historical evidence. *The Sports Historian, 19*(1), 16–37. doi: 10.1080/17460269909445806

Malcolm, D. (2001). "It's not cricket": Colonial legacies and contemporary inequalities. *Journal of Historical Sociology, 14*(3), 253–275. doi: 10.1111/1467-6443.00146

Marshall, N. A. (2012). A clinician's guide to recognizing and reporting parental psychological maltreatment of children. *Professional Psychology: Research and Practice, 43*(2), 73–79. doi: 10.1037/a0026677

Martin, A. (2016). *MCC recommends sendings off be introduced into laws of cricket.* Retrieved from www.theguardian.com/sport/2016/dec/07/mcc-recommend-red-cards-sending-off-laws-of-cricket

Rayner, M., Webb, T., & Webb, H. (2016). The occurrence of referee abuse in rugby union: Evidence and measures through an online survey. *The International Journal of Sports Management, Recreation and Tourism, 21*(d). http://dx.doi.org/10.5199/ijsmart-1791-874X-21d

Referee Development Day Presentation. (2017). The Football Association.

Richards, H. (2006). *A game for hooligans: The history of rugby union.* London: Mainstream Publishing.

Ridinger, L. L., Kim, K. R., Warner, S., & Tingle, J. K. (2017a). Development of the referee retention scale. *Journal of Sport Management, 31*(5), 514–527. http://dx.doi.org/10.1123/jsm.2017-0065

Ridinger, L. L., Warner, S., Tingle, J. K., & Kim, K. R. (2017b). Why referees stay in the game. *Global Sport Business Journal, 5*(3), 22–37.

Stirling, A. E. (2009). Definition and constituents of maltreatment in sport: Establishing a conceptual framework for research practitioners. *British Journal of Sports Medicine, 43*(14), 1091–1099. doi: 10.1136/bjsm.2008.051433

Stirling, A. E. (2013). Understanding the use of emotionally abusive coaching practices. *International Journal of Sports Science & Coaching, 8*(4), 625–639. doi: 10.1260/1747-9541.8.4.625

Stirling, A. E., & Kerr, G. A. (2008a). Defining and categorizing emotional abuse in sport. *European Journal of Sport Science, 8*(4), 173–181. doi: 10.1080/17461390802086281

Stirling, A. E., & Kerr, G. A. (2008b). Elite female swimmers' experiences of emotional abuse across time. *Journal of Emotional Abuse, 7*(4), 89–113. doi: 10.1300/J135v07n04_05

Stirling, A. E., & Kerr, G. A. (2013). The perceived effects of elite athletes' experiences of emotional abuse in the coach-athlete relationship. *International Journal of Sport and Exercise Psychology, 11*(1), 87–100. doi: 10.1080/1612197X.2013.752173

Swanson, B. (2018). *Pierluigi Collina warns of a global shortage of referees if abuse is not acted upon.* Retrieved October 22, 2018, from www.skysports.com/football/news/11095/10810551/pierluigi-collina-warns-of-a-global-shortage-of-referees-if-abuse-is-not-acted-upon

Tenenbaum, G., Singer, R. N., Stewart, E., & Duda, J. (1997). Aggression and violence in sport: An ISSP position stand. *The Sport Psychologist, 11*(1), 1–7. doi: 10.1123/tsp.11.1.1

Vamplew, W. (1980). Sport crowd disorder in Britain, 1870–1914: Causes and controls. *Journal of Sport History, 7*(1), 5–20.

Wann, D. L., Carlson, J. D., & Schrader, M. P. (1999). The impact of team identification on the hostile and instrumental verbal aggression of sport spectators. *Journal of Social Behavior and Personality, 14*(2), 279–286.

Warner, S., Tingle, J. K., & Kellett, P. (2013). Officiating attrition: The experiences of former referees via a sport development lens. *Journal of Sport Management, 27*(4), 316–328. doi: 10.1123/jsm.27.4.316

Webb, T. (2016). "Knight of the whistle": W. P. Harper and the impact of the media on an association football referee. *The International Journal of the History of Sport, 33*(3), 306–324. doi: 10.1080/09523367.2016.1151004

Webb, T. (2017). *Elite soccer referees: Officiating in the Premier League, La Liga and Serie A.* London: Routledge.

Webb, T. (2018). Managing match officials: The influence of business and the impact of finance in the Premier League era. In S. Chadwick, D. Parnell, P. Widdop, & C. Anagnostopoulos (Eds.), *Routledge handbook of football business and management* (pp. 366–375). London: Routledge.

Webb, T., Cleland, J., & O'Gorman, J. (2017). The distribution of power through a media campaign: The respect programme, referees and violence in association football. *The Journal of Global Sport Management, 2*(3), 162–181. doi: 10.1080/24704067.2017.1350591

Webb, T., Dicks, M., Thelwell, R., Van der Kamp, G. J., & Rix-Lievre, G. (2020). An analysis of soccer referee experiences in France and the Netherlands: Abuse, conflict, and level of support. *Sport Management Review, 23*(1), 52–65. doi: 10.1016/j.smr.2019.03.003

Webb, T., & Rayner, M. (2016). Sportsmanship from a referee's perspective: A case study of four sports. In T. Delaney (Ed.), *Sportsmanship: Multi-disciplinary perspectives* (pp. 162–172). Jefferson, North Carolina, USA: McFarland Publishing.

Webb, T., Rayner, M., & Thelwell, R. (2018). An explorative case study of referee abuse in English Rugby League. *Journal of Applied Sport Management, 10*(2). doi: 10.18666/JASM-2017-V10-12-8834

Webb, T., Rayner, M., & Thelwell, R. (2019). An examination of match official's perceptions of support and abuse in rugby union and cricket in England. *Managing Sport and Leisure, 24*(1–3), 155–172. doi: 10.1080/23750472.2019.1605841

2 Examining abuse

The importance of governing bodies in sport

Introduction

This chapter explores the nature and scale of abuse experienced by sports officials across different levels of sports in England. It initially examines the current literature concerning match official abuse, the support that exists for match officials and any issues with this provision, the reasons for match official discontinuation and potential strategies to address any discontinuation. Following this, the chapter utilises descriptive statistics from the previously mentioned online surveys (see Chapter 1), followed by qualitative data from the surveys where match officials were encouraged to elaborate on their initial responses to questions on the support networks that exist, the abuse to which they have been subjected and their experiences when reporting any incidents of abuse. These responses provide examples of particular verbal and physical abusive situations, the settings for these incidents and the actors (players, coaches and spectators) involved. Finally, this chapter then considers how match officials deal with and attempt to manage abusive actions and behaviour towards them.

Abuse and retention across sports

Abuse and issues such as the retention of match officials can be considered across many different sports. The abuse of rugby union match officials, for example, has been examined through a pilot study across three counties in England, discovering that verbal and physical abuse has increased, with 40% of referees reporting that they have been subjected to abuse in the last two years (Rayner, Webb, & Webb, 2016). Furthermore, research emanating from England has also identified that insufficient consideration of the support, development and management of referees could lead to further declines in participation numbers, given the support and mediation required to resolve any form of conflict (Rayner et al., 2016; Webb, Rayner, & Thelwell, 2018).

Other sports spanning different countries have displayed similar trends to sports in England with regards to the treatment of sports match officials by players, coaches and spectators, and the conflict which can occur. In Australia and the United States, sports such as basketball, Australian Rules football, baseball and lacrosse have tackled matters regarding the retention of their match officials (sports outside England are considered in greater detail in Chapter 6). Studies have identified requirements to increase match official recruitment and encourage match officials to be retained in their chosen sport, recognising the importance of community and social interaction, administration and training in the retention of match officials (Kellett & Warner, 2011; Ridinger, 2015; Warner, Tingle, & Kellett, 2013). In addition, Australian Rules football umpires have identified that they routinely receive abuse and that this abuse is seen as a 'normal' part of their role. Such findings indicate an acceptance of conflict and that the socialisation and interaction of umpires can contribute to their retention within Australian Rules football (Kellett & Shilbury, 2007).

The work of Kellett and Shilbury (2007) in relation to Australian Rules Football umpires (see also Kellett & Warner, 2011), and other scholars in lacrosse (Ridinger, 2015), basketball (Warner et al., 2013), football (Cleland, O'Gorman, & Webb, 2018; Webb, Dicks, Thelwell, Van der Kamp, & Rix-Lievre, 2019), rugby union (Rayner et al., 2016; Webb, Rayner, & Thelwell, 2019), rugby league (Webb et al., 2018) and cricket (Webb et al., 2019), have all identified that conflict can contribute to match officials' experiences of stress in their chosen sports, leading to pressures inside and outside the playing area (Selcuk, 2009). Therefore, stress has been highlighted as a direct consequence of officiating, also having a profound impact on mental health, the performance of match officials and dropout intentions (Belkacem & Salih, 2018). This is a topic we cover in more detail in Chapter 5.

Voight (2009, p. 91) identified particular areas as scoring highly for stress amongst match officials, namely "conflict between officiating and family demands", "making a controversial call" and "conflict between officiating and work demands". Stress-related research has also been undertaken with ice hockey match officials. This research considered the source and intensity of their experience of stressful events. The three most prevalent stressors identified in particular were "making a controversial call", "difficulty working with a partner official" and "confrontation with coaches" (Dorsch & Paskevich, 2007, p. 589). In addition to these stressors, the fear of mistakes and verbal and physical abuse was also found to exist and differ across levels of officiating. For example, the lowest level of ice hockey officials experienced less stress, whilst the stress from the fear of making mistakes was greater than that from incidents of abuse. Perhaps unsurprisingly, the importance of intervention programmes to deal effectively with difficult situations or conflicts which the match officials might experience were also highlighted (Dorsch & Paskevich, 2007).

Abuse in England: governing body approaches

It is important before considering incidents of abuse, to focus upon the extent of abuse towards match officials in England, before turning to sports in other countries (see Chapter 6). Historically considered as traditional sports with much of their grounding in England, both rugby union and cricket are sports widely considered to contain an acceptance of and an ethos towards sportsmanship (Webb & Rayner, 2016). This acknowledgement of sportsmanship and the acceptance of the rules and also the authority of the match official are considered inherent in both rugby union and cricket (Collins, 2009; Dunning & Sheard, 2005).

The Rugby Football Union (RFU) has identified and acknowledged a growing concern related to the abuse of their referees, a subject also documented and analysed through academic research (Rayner et al., 2016; Webb et al., 2019). As such, in 2018 the RFU launched an initiative entitled "keep your boots on", with the overarching aim of upholding rugby's values, advising that the protection of referees was now a strategic priority for the organisation, as they react to a changing sporting landscape (Keep your boots on, 2018). Meanwhile, the Rugby Football League (RFL) also reacted to the abuse of their referees at varying levels of the game, by considering the impact that this abuse, and the pressure of their role, might have on the individual referees (Bower, 2018; Webb et al., 2018).

In addition, in 2016 the Marylebone Cricket Club (MCC) commenced trials designed to curb on-field violence, both towards other players as well as umpires. The trials included, amongst other things, the introduction of red cards for the most extreme incidents of on-field behaviour and enabling the umpires to send players from the field of play, an action which they had not previously been afforded (Clough, 2016). Following the successful trials, and against a backdrop of increased, sustained violence and abuse, the MCC decided to implement the red card sending-off procedure and award penalty runs for poor behaviour (Martin, 2016).

The updated laws came into effect globally from 1 October 2017, and the MCC detailed four descending levels of offences and corresponding punishment. Level 1, for example, includes actions such as excessive appealing and showing dissent towards an umpire's decision, with punishment starting at an official warning, and a second offence resulting in five penalty runs. Level 4, however, includes actions such as threatening an umpire and any other act of violence on the field of play, and the punishment for such actions is the removal of the offending player from the field of play for the remainder of the match (Hytner, 2017).

In England, the FA designed and implemented a public information campaign to raise awareness of the deleterious impact of abusive behaviour towards match officials by a range of football stakeholders. Delivered as a 'top-down' initiative by those in managerial or strategic employment positions (Sabatier, 1986), the Respect Programme, introduced in 2008 (The FA, 2008), aimed to assist referees in their match-to-match operation and performance, as referees were facing a worsening situation, and the general environment around football matches was believed to be a concern. The Respect Programme began by initially identifying grassroots or mass participation football as the setting for change, utilising codes of conduct, online videos, adverts and pitch side barriers for parents and spectators to remain behind during matches (Cleland, O'Gorman, & Bond, 2015). It targeted the entire referee population in England irrespective of their operational level, seeking to change the behaviour of players, spectators and parents through the dissemination of knowledge, all with the overarching aim of increasing the recruitment and retention of referees (Cleland et al., 2015; Cleland et al., 2018). The programme was devised to tackle wider issues across the game, such as referees discontinuing, and the fact that referees were not being recruited in enough numbers (The FA, 2008). The FA recognised that poor behaviour was having a detrimental impact on the game at every playing level from elite sport to grassroots leagues, demonstrated with a loss of 17% or just under 5,000 active referees from the 2007–2008 to 2008–2009 season due, at least in part, to abuse from players and spectators (Brackenridge, Pitchford, &Wilson, 2011; The FA, 2008).

Despite the national coverage of the Respect Programme referees are still subjected to excessive levels of abuse. Although the Respect Programme is designed as a 'top down' public information campaign, there is little evidence to support the effectiveness of campaigns of this nature in sport or wider afield (Cleland et al., 2015). Added to the concerns of the implementation of a top down campaign, there was a lack of awareness among those groups that the Respect Programme is targeted towards, such as referees, coaches, spectators and players (Elliott & Drummond, 2015; Lusted & O'Gorman, 2010).

The success of the Respect Programme has been a topic of focus, both within the national media (Keogh, 2018; Wilson, 2016, 2018) and also throughout academic research (Cleland et al., 2015; Cleland et al., 2018; Webb, Cleland, & O'Gorman, 2017). Despite the introduction of the Respect Programme, there has continued to be issues related to the abuse of referees, both verbal and physical in nature. The FA refreshed the Respect Programme in 2018, launching a strapline entitled "we only do positive" (The FA, n.d.), and in 2019 the FA began promoting a 21-day period of positivity incorporating information and suggested actions for clubs to strengthen relationships within their teams, creating a long-lasting and positive environment for the players.

The original objectives of the Respect Programme were:

- To recruit and retain enough referees for the demands of the game at every level.
- To reduce the number of assaults on referees.
- To achieve an improvement in on-field player discipline particularly in the area of dissent to referees.
- To manage a step change in youth football as to what is acceptable and unacceptable behaviour from parents and spectators.

(Hampshire FA, n.d.)

The initiative also targets parents, their behaviour around the playing area, as well as encouraging their wider involvement in the club (The FA, 2019).

Given actions taken by governing bodies in attempting to reduce abuse, as well as the academic literature highlighting some of the issues across sports (Cleland et al., 2018; Rayner et al., 2016; Webb et al., 2019; Webb et al., 2017), it is clear that a more detailed understanding of the issue is required. From an academic position, we introduce findings from a range of surveys in England here related to the extent and frequency of abuse to which match officials are exposed, as well as specific accounts from match officials, in order to further examine the extent and settings for any abusive situations. As Figure 2.1 demonstrates, the extent of abuse differs from sport to sport, with 53.7% of rugby union referees surveyed stating they had been verbally abused, whereas 56.5% of cricket umpires surveyed had been verbally abused. However, 93.7% of football and 85.4% of rugby league

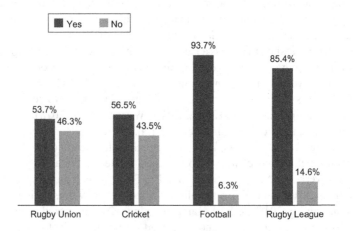

Figure 2.1 Have you been verbally abused?

match officials surveyed reported greater levels of verbal abuse, emphasising some of the issues which led the FA to launch the Respect Programme and for the RFL to consider the impact of abuse on the match officials.

The extent of abuse towards match officials

The level of verbal abuse across each of the four sports demonstrates concerns for the respective governing bodies. This concern should also exist for the level of physical abuse that is experienced by match officials as demonstrated in Figure 2.2:

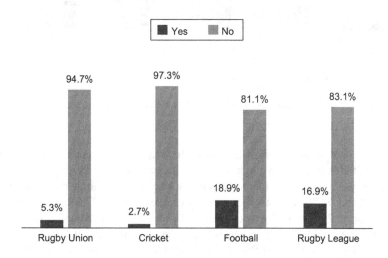

Figure 2.2 Have you been physically abused?

These findings across sports in England present a disturbing trend of both verbal and physical abuse experiences by match officials, with all four sports showing that over 50% have been subjected to verbal abuse at some point in their career. Physical abuse is much less prevalent, although there is an argument to suggest that any physical abuse or verbal abuse of a match official in any sport is unacceptable. Figure 2.2 shows that football and rugby league demonstrate the greater number of match officials who experience this physical abuse. Rugby union has more physically abusive incidents than cricket, although neither sport is close to football and rugby league in this regard.

Figure 2.3, meanwhile, outlines and compares the frequency of the abuse to which match officials are subjected in England, with clear distinctions evident between the sports, as we also saw when comparing sports in Figures 2.1 and 2.2.

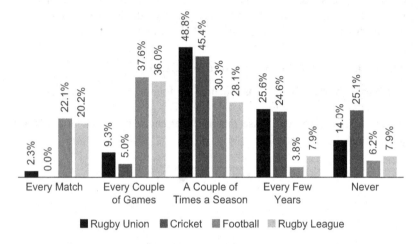

Figure 2.3 How often do you receive what you would consider to be abuse?

There are considerable differences in the frequency or regularity of abuse across the four sports in England. Figure 2.3 shows that a far greater number of match officials in football and rugby league receive abuse every game, 22.1% and 20.2% respectively, and every couple of games, 37.6% and 36.0%. In contrast, 2.3% of rugby union match officials and 0% of cricket match officials have reported that they receive abuse every match, and 9.3% of rugby union match officials and 5% of cricket umpires receive abuse every couple of games. However, a significant proportion of both rugby union and cricket match officials stated that they receive abuse a couple of times a season, demonstrating a level of regularity of abuse towards match officials and a potential impact upon match officials deciding to leave their roles. Given the historic issues with abuse towards match officials, particularly evident in football, the regularity of the abuse shows that the issues have not been effectively resolved.

Abuse in action

One of the consequences of abuse towards match officials can be their discontinuation from their respective sport. There can be other contributory factors, although abuse is found to be a primary factor in this discontinuation (Cleland et al., 2018; Ridinger, 2015; Warner, Tingle, & Kellett, 2013; Webb et al., 2017, 2019). The concept of match official discontinuation is considered further in Chapter 4, when we discuss the consequences of abuse when related to support networks. However, it is important to understand in detail how this abuse manifests itself and in order to do this we present accounts from match officials of the personal experiences they have encountered in their different sports.

First, it is important to establish the context of abuse and the settings in which it can manifest within a match official's working environment. Jacobs, Tingle, Oja, and Smith (2020) suggest that abuse is a verbal statement or physical act, which implies or threatens physical harm to a referee or a referee's property. Furthermore, Chiafullo (1998) notes that abuse includes (but is not limited to) the following acts committed on a referee: using foul or abusive language, throwing any beverage on a referee's personal property or verbally threatening a referee. What is evident in research like this is that abuse can occur and be measured at all stages of a match official's working environment regardless of the sport, age or sex of the official. However, what are less well known are the exact settings and triggers for these abusive environments.

Folkesson, Nyberg, Archer, and Norlander (2002) examined the environments relating to threats and aggression received by football match officials in the Varmland Football Association, Sweden. Their research identified sources of aggression emanating from players, coaches and spectators towards the match officials. While Folkesson et al.'s (2002) work identifies the groups that deliver the torrents of abuse towards referees, these groups are not isolated within football and are evidenced across sports as the following quote illustrates:

> I have experienced abuse on numerous occasions. I have sent quite a few people off for abuse directed at me . . . I have been threatened with physical abuse on a few occasions and received abuse from players, coaches and spectators.
>
> (Rugby league referee, male, 3–5 years'
> experience, under 18 age group)

Consistently evidenced within research conducted by Cleland et al. (2018), Folkesson et al. (2002), Ridinger, (2015), Warner et al. (2013), Webb et al. (2017), and Webb et al. (2020) is that abuse is triggered when thoughts and opinions of players, coaches and spectators conflict with the decisions made by the match official within a game context. This was further illustrated by this cricket umpire, amongst others in the data, (male, 11–15 years' experience, 55–64 age group) who explained:

> I have experienced a very small amount of mild verbal abuse from both batsmen and bowlers. This is always on the turning down of an appeal by bowlers and on dismissal of a batsman. I cannot recall this being personal in nature, more expressions of frustration coupled with some choice expletives! "You've got to be f . . . ing joking".

The triggers of abuse based on decisions made by the match official is not a new phenomenon, however these incidences have increased over the last few decades across a number of sports. The concept of disagreeing with a match official's decision is often noted as an emotional reaction rather than a pre-conceived response. Some of the possible explanations for this increase in abuse towards the match official have been framed around a lack of subject knowledge from both the perpetrators of abuse and the match official. These incidents are from multiple players, over a prolonged period of time during the game and directed specifically at the on-field official, meaning that the management of players on the field of play becomes more difficult for the official and the captains of the teams. As outlined by this cricket umpire (male, 2 years or less experience, 55–64 age group):

> These instances ranged from protracted dissent against my decisions by the fielding side, swearing aimed in my direction by one or more players and captains failing to manage their team's conduct on the field.

Research has illustrated that match officials undergo a range of physiological, psychological and technical training in order to perform in their working environments (Webb, 2017). Nonetheless, while there are coaching courses and public access to varying levels of sport through a range of media, none of the perpetrators of abuse undergo such rigorous and continuous training as the match officials on the laws and regulations of sport. This means that unsporting or abusive behaviour goes unchallenged, and it becomes extremely difficult to affect the behaviour of players, coaches and spectators.

Next we further consider examples of abuse towards match officials across sports, and the similarities in the challenges faced by match officials irrespective of the sport involved. This abuse is outlined and explained in relation to the four different sports in England from which data were collected. The examples of abuse highlight the issues that currently exist, with match officials describing players, coaches and spectators as distinct groups who direct abuse towards them.

Match official abuse in sport

As demonstrated earlier in this chapter, football has high levels of verbal and physical abuse towards match officials. One football referee (male, 16–20 years' experience, 45–54 age group) exemplified the problems faced on a regular basis:

> Unsporting behaviour is an in-built culture and regarded by managers, coaches and players as their right and opportunity to express themselves

in a very underhand, undermining demeanor towards referees . . . the notice that hangs on the walls within football changing rooms asking all clubs, players and officials to adhere to the protocol and parameters striving to keep in check and avoid football abuse, is merely displayed as lip service. I would say county level, Saturday football is probably the worst example of players using every conceivable way to win, whatever it takes. Abuse, cheap comments towards officials and a general want to shout foul for almost every contact . . . red and yellow cards have not thwarted the wall of abuse and unsporting action is seen week in week out around the UK. Right now, no campaign, not even the Respect campaign [sic] has had any real sustainable effect.

The regularity of the abuse identified in this quote, and the fact that the abuse is considered "an in-built culture" with stakeholders such as players, coaches and managers considering that this an acceptable way to behave in football is concerning. The description of reducing abuse as "lip service" is also troubling, given the importance of a unified approach, such as the Respect Programme and the lack of sustainable impact that the programme has been able to maintain. Other football referees have identified issues in youth football. Although the Respect Programme has undoubtedly made gains since its introduction, there are still concerns around the behaviour of coaches, and referees have identified links between behaviour in the professional game and what happens at a local level:

What annoys me is the amount and level of abuse. In youth football kids unfortunately are exposed to bad role models from the adults involved. It's also the professionals and it goes down the levels to amateurs and youth football. The children see the behaviour on television, and they think if their hero's doing it, or if they see their dad doing it on the touchline then it's ok . . . they just don't accept decisions from referees. It's one of the reasons that I stopped refereeing. There's a huge shortage of referees. We could end up with no referees.

(Football referee, male, 10 years'
experience, 35–44 age group)

The link between the professional game and the behaviour of players, coaches and spectators in the grassroots game, particularly in youth football, is perceived by this referee and others in our sample to expose young players to examples of poor behaviour. The link is also made between abuse and the discontinuation of football referees, with particular reference made to the inability of professional players to accept the decisions of the referee, and the imitation of this behaviour by young players during the game.

Other referees also identified the link between television, poor player behaviour at the elite level and the exposure of this behaviour through extensive television coverage. This coverage permits the increasingly regular broadcast of football matches, and the resultant incidents that occur during the match:

> Players still swear at referees. It doesn't get dealt with at the top on TV so why should we expect amateur players to behave any different? Too many teams/players go into a football game with aggressive attitudes looking to intimidate opponents and referees, and they are allowed to get away with it even when reported.
>
> (Football referee, male, 2 years or less experience, 25–34 age group)

The issues of teams and players acting aggressively, and perhaps as importantly, being permitted to "get away with it" in the eyes of the referees, means that this intimidation towards other players and referees will continue. Other football referees also believed that there was a mob mentality that existed on the touchlines. For example, this referee (female, 2 years or less experience, 45–54 age group), amongst many from our sample, identified that in her experience parents and coaches in youth football as individuals were generally positive and reasonable, but not when they merge as a group on a match day:

> I do find even now that either a team, its coaches and parents are reasonable as a whole group or they are not. It appears to me that if one of the spectators, be it coach or parent, is vociferous then they all seem to be and join in. I have had games where one side of spectators and coaches were shouting across the pitch their disagreement to the other side – it was ridiculous. There are still frequent games where it is a continuous challenge from the side lines of every decision.

The issue is when one coach or parent begins to vocally question the decision or performance of the referee it can lead to other parents imitating this behaviour, and therefore the behaviour deteriorating into some form of abuse.

However, this is a situation that is not just unique to football. Rugby union referees outlined similar experiences in terms of abuse and the behaviour of players, coaches and spectators. Some referees identified coaches at Colts level to be a particular problem, whereas other referees believed that it is coaches and supporters more widely that are the issue. One referee explained that the "biggest concern is the poor standards of pitch side behaviour set by coaches of junior and colts side" (male, 11–15 years' experience,

45–54 age group), whilst another referee (male, 11–15 years' experience, 55–64 age group) questioned how those in positions of governance could combat the problem:

> The level of abuse is higher from coaches and supporters (parents in junior games), I don't really see what can be done to deal with this. Coaches can be reprimanded, of course and even banned, but that won't change their mentality. Supporters cannot be controlled.

The pitch side behaviour of coaches and supporters is a concern which rugby union referees perceived as a developing and ongoing issue. Rugby union referees believed that it should be the duty of the clubs to discourage any abusive behaviour. The fact that referees understood that it was difficult for the RFU, for example, to control supporters and that it was a difficult situation to deal with, means that clubs should be more accountable in trying to tackle this problem. As explained by one referee, this can subsequently have a deleterious effect on the enjoyment of referees, particularly at a community or local level:

> Players are informed we are there to enjoy their games as much as they do, especially in junior games where far too many parents are trying to re-live their youth through their children. We always seem to receive the blame for everything that goes wrong in the game, rather than the players.
>
> (Rugby union referee, male, 16–20 years'
> experience, 55–64 age group)

This reduction in enjoyment for rugby union referees is troubling for those in positions of governance, with any reduction in enjoyment potentially impacting the retention of referees (as discussed further in Chapter 3). In order to address some of the issues raised, referees believed that clubs, in particular, need to take more responsibility for the behaviour of their players and that there should be associated punishments to deter abuse towards match officials. One rugby union referee (male, 11–15 years' experience, 55–64 age group) believed that increasing punishments would assist in averting the increasing abuse received by referees:

> More punitive and preventative actions by clubs and societies in respect of referee abuse. Clubs are not taking enough responsibility within their own ranks to deal with the matter at the time of the incident. As an older referee, I recollect times when anyone verbally abusing a referee would be taken to task by their own club mates on the touchline. A return to better values is required otherwise referees will leave the game

Responses like this were also raised by cricket umpires who identified that rather than the clubs, it is the leagues in which the clubs play that are more important in the disciplinary process: "I have reported several players over the years for verbal abuse – they were dealt with by the League rather than by the ECB", said one cricket umpire (male, 11–15 years' experience, 65+ age group), whilst another (male, 2 years or less experience, 35–44 age group) identified that the leagues (although involved in disciplinary procedures) need to be more stringent when it comes to punishments: "Some other leagues need to take a stronger approach to discipline and the spirit of cricket". Despite the demand for more action from the leagues, an acceptance of bad language towards match officials within cricket, similar to that in rugby union, from coaches/managers was recognised as a concern, as was the normalisation of this type of language used towards them. By way of illustration, this cricket umpire (male, 16–20 years' experience, 55–64 age group) stated: "One problem I encountered was the attitude of managers who argued that 'it was just the use of work place language' and 'we should not be that upset by it'".

The normalisation of abusive language towards cricket umpires demonstrates a change in terms of the acceptance of negative behaviour. This view is also taken in rugby league, with some referees stating that verbal abuse is expected and that this abuse can be extremely personal in nature, but often came from spectators. As one referee (male, 21+ years' experience, 35–44 age group) described: "Verbal abuse tends to be mainly from off-field spectators than anyone on field", whilst another referee (male, 6–10 years' experience, 18–24 age group) stated: "The culture of referees is that verbal abuse is expected, including homophobic abuse".

Conclusion

Clearly, abusive incidents are prevalent across the four English sports examined here, albeit at different levels. For example, we have presented evidence of verbal abuse in football, cricket, rugby union and rugby league as well as evidence of physical abuse, particularly in football and rugby league. The issue of abuse towards match officials is not a recent concern; in fact it has been a problem for governing bodies over a prolonged period of time. In particular, historical issues in football are still prevalent in the game today, such as abuse from crowds or spectators at matches towards referees. Given that these matters are ongoing, it is important for governing bodies to address the concerns of match officials and prevent increased match official attrition rates.

Match officials cited concerns around diminishing enjoyment when they officiate due to regular and prolonged abuse from players, coaches and spectators, with the behaviour of spectators and coaches on the edge of the playing area described as very challenging at times. There were also observations which identified a lack of collective action aimed at tackling the abuse to which match officials are subjected across the four sports. Leagues and clubs were discussed and their role in challenging negative behaviour towards match officials requires some attention from those in positions of governance at the national governing bodies. Perhaps the most perturbing aspect of the abuse described by the match officials from the different sports is the perception that this abuse is ingrained, that it is part of the very cultural fabric of the respective gameday routine. Challenging and changing this ingrained culture will take time, strong governance and financial investment. These are all facets which will require input and drive from governing bodies, leagues and clubs in order for the landscape to change. It will not be achieved without this collaborative approach.

The next chapter examines the support and guidance offered by the respective governing bodies in England and the processes and procedures that are in place for match officials to report any abusive incidents to which they have been exposed. We examine these issues across the four English sports and consider any implications for match officials and also governing body administrators, given the importance of their role in supporting, training and developing match officials.

References

Belkacem, C., & Salih, K. (2018). The relationship between the sources of psychological stress and the level of self-esteem among football referees. *European Journal of Physical Education and Sport Science*, 3(12), 575–593. http://dx.doi.org/10.5281/zenodo.1145469

Bower, A. (2018). *From drugs and alcohol to wellbeing: How rugby league is tackling mental health*. Retrieved from www.theguardian.com/sport/2018/jun/14/state-of-mind-rugby-league-mental-health

Brackenridge, C., Pitchford, A., & Wilson, M. (2011). Respect: Results of a pilot project designed to improve behaviour in English football. *Managing Leisure*, 16(3), 175–191. doi: 10.1080/13606719.2011.583406

Chiafullo, C. M. (1998). From personal foul to personal attack: How sports officials are the target of physical abuse from players, coaches and fans alike. *Seton Hall Journal of Sports and Entertainment Law, 8*, 201–225.

Cleland, J., O'Gorman, J., & Bond, M. (2015). The English football association's respect campaign: The referees' view. *International Journal of Sport, Policy and Politics, 7*(4), 551–563. doi: 10.1080/19406940.2015.1088050

Cleland, J., O'Gorman, J., & Webb, T. (2018). Respect? An investigation into the experience of referees in association football. *International Review for the Sociology of Sport, 53*(8), 960–974. doi: 10.1177/1012690216687979

Clough, D. (2016). *Cricket to introduce red cards for "most extreme" on-field behaviour.* Retrieved from www.independent.co.uk/sport/cricket/red-cards-mcc-laws-of-cricket-a7460246.html

Collins, T. (2009). *A social history of English rugby union.* London: Routledge.

Dorsch, K. D., & Paskevich, D. M. (2007). Stressful experiences among six certification levels of ice hockey officials. *Psychology of Sport and Exercise, 8*(4), 585–593. doi: 10.1016/j.psychsport.2006.06.003

Dunning, E., & Sheard, K. (2005). *Barbarians, gentlemen and players: A sociological study of rugby football.* London: Routledge.

Elliott, S., & Drummond, M. (2015). The (limited) impact of sport policy on parental behaviour in youth sport: A qualitative inquiry in junior Australian football. *International Journal of Sport Policy and Politics, 7*(4), 519–530. doi: 10.1080/19406940.2014.971850

The FA. (2008). *The FA's vision: 2008–2012.* London: The FA.

The FA. (2019). *Registration for this year's 21 days of positivity is now open.* Retrieved from www.thefa.com/get-involved/respect/21-days-of-positivity

The FA. (n.d.). *Respect.* Retrieved from www.thefa.com/get-involved/respect

Folkesson, P., Nyberg, C., Archer, T., & Norlander, T. (2002). Soccer referees' experience of threat and aggression: Effects of age, experience, and life orientation on outcome of coping strategy. *Aggressive Behavior: Official Journal of the International Society for Research on Aggression, 28*(4), 317–327. doi: 10.1002/ab.90028

Hampshire FA. (n.d.). *Respect.* Retrieved from www.hampshirefa.com/about/respect

Hytner, M. (2017). *Sendings off and limitations to bat size to be introduced to laws of cricket.* Retrieved from www.theguardian.com/sport/2017/mar/07/limitations-on-bat-size-and-sendings-off-to-be-introduced-to-laws-of-cricket

Jacobs, B. L., Tingle, J. K., Oja, B. D., & Smith, M. A. (2020). Exploring referee abuse through the lens of the collegiate rugby coach. *Sport Management Review, 23*(1), 39–51. doi: 10.1016/j.smr.2019.03.004

Keep your boots on. (2018). *Respect for referees.* Retrieved from https://keepyourbootson.co.uk/respect-for-referees/

Kellett, P., & Shilbury, D. (2007). Umpire participation: Is abuse really the issue? *Sport Management Review, 10*(3), 209–229. doi: 10.1016/S1441-3523(07)70012-8

Kellett, P., & Warner, S. (2011). Creating communities that lead to retention: The social worlds and communities of umpires. *European Sport Management Quarterly, 11*(5), 471–494. doi: 10.1080/16184742.2011.624109

Keogh, F. (2018). *Referee's jaw broken after attack in Irish amateur league.* Retrieved from www.bbc.co.uk/sport/football/46180452

Lusted, J., & O'Gorman, J. (2010). The impact of new labour's modernisation agenda on the English grass-roots football workforce. *Managing Leisure, 15*(1–2), 140–154. doi: 10.1080/13606710903448236

Martin, A. (2016). *MCC recommends sendings off be introduced into laws of cricket.* Retrieved from www.theguardian.com/sport/2016/dec/07/mcc-recommend-red-cards-sending-off-laws-of-cricket

Rayner, M., Webb, T., & Webb, H. (2016). The occurrence of referee abuse in rugby union: Evidence and measures through an online survey. *The International*

Journal of Sports Management, Recreation and Tourism, 21(d). http://dx.doi.org/10.5199/ijsmart-1791-874X-21d

Ridinger, L. (2015). Contributors and constraints to involvement with youth sports officiating. *Journal of Amateur Sport, 1*(2), 103–127. doi: 10.17161/jas.v1i2.4946

Sabatier, P. A. (1986). Top-down and bottom-up approaches to implementation research: A critical analysis and suggested synthesis. *Journal of Public Policy, 6*(1), 21–48. doi: 10.1017/S0143814X00003846

Selcuk, G. (2009). Magnitude of psychological stress reported by soccer referees. *Social Behaviour and Personality: An International Journal, 37*(7), 865–868. doi: 10.2224/sbp.2009.37.7.865

Voight, M. (2009). Sources of stress and coping strategies of US soccer officials. *Stress & Health, 25*(1), 91–101. doi: 10.1002/smi.1231

Warner, S., Tingle, J. K., & Kellett, P. (2013). Officiating attrition: The experiences of former referees via a sport development lens. *Journal of Sport Management, 27*(4), 316–328. doi: 10.1123/jsm.27.4.316

Webb, T., Cleland, J., & O'Gorman, J. (2017). The distribution of power through a media campaign: The respect programme, referees and violence in association football. *The Journal of Global Sport Management, 2*(3), 162–181. doi: 10.1080/24704067.2017.1350591

Webb, T., Rayner, M. & Thelwell, R. (2019). An examination of match official's perceptions of support and abuse in rugby union and cricket in England. *Managing Sport and Leisure, 24*(1-3), 155-172

Webb, T., Dicks, M., Thelwell, R., Van der Kamp, G. J., & Rix-Lievre, G. (2020). An analysis of soccer referee experiences in France and the Netherlands: Abuse, conflict, and support. *Sport Management Review, 23*(1), 52–65. doi: 10.1016/j.smr.2019.03.003

Webb, T., & Rayner, M. (2016). Sportsmanship from a referee's perspective: A case study of four sports. In T. Delaney (Ed.), *Sportsmanship: Multi-disciplinary perspectives* (pp. 162–172). Jefferson, North Carolina, USA: McFarland Publishing.

Webb, T., Rayner, M., & Thelwell, R. (2018). An explorative case study of referee abuse in English Rugby League. *Journal of Applied Sport Management, 10*(2). doi: 10.18666/JASM-2017-V10-12-8834

Wilson, J. (2016). *Exclusive: Football demands end to the growing menace of abuse against referees.* Retrieved from www.telegraph.co.uk/football/2016/03/22/football-unites-to-fight-growing-menace-of-abuse-against-referee/

Wilson, J. (2018). *English football officials seven times more likely to be verbally abused than European counterparts.* Retrieved from www.telegraph.co.uk/football/2018/12/20/english-football-officials-seven-times-likely-verbally-abused/

3 Organisational culture, non-reporting of abuse and discontinuation

Implications for match officials and administrators

Introduction

Match officials operate within a curious space in sport. Governing bodies oversee the development, finances and structure of the game; leagues and cup competitions provide a competitive platform for teams to participate; and match officials are required to uphold and maintain the laws of the game within these contexts. The sports we focus upon in this book, namely football, cricket, rugby union and rugby league all provide these organisational elements, although each has its own particular structures and operational requirements. Of course, these structures are also affected by the professional games that exist in each of the sports in question, the money available to develop both grassroots sport and the professional game, and consequently the financial infrastructure invested in match officials as a distinct group of people within their chosen sport.

The training match officials require is different to that required by players, and the organisation of them as a group is unique. Consequently, unique demands are placed on governing bodies and administrators of different sports that need to be understood in order to successfully manage, support and develop match officials effectively (Webb, Wagstaff, Rayner, & Thelwell, 2016). Many of these organisational, leadership and management facets can be applied across sports, and therefore areas of good practice and aspects that require improvement in any sport can help to shed light on the current situational requirements for match officials. Good governance, effective leadership and management, as well as strong and identifiable organisational cultures can all contribute towards more content match officials.

Therefore, this chapter utilises the survey data gathered from football, cricket, rugby union and rugby league match officials in England to examine the extent to which organisational culture mediates the match officials' individual and group behaviour, experiences of management and leadership of their roles, and the impact these factors can have on the performance of match officials at varying levels of their sports. In order to do this, further findings from our research are considered and related back to the extant literature in order to explore and understand the current landscape in sport.

Organisational culture

We can trace the origination of the study and scholarly analysis of organisational culture in sport to the late 1970s (Pettigrew, 1979; Trice & Beyer, 1984). Maitland, Hills, and Rhind (2015) argue that although the concept of organisational culture has been defined, it is investigated and analysed in different ways by researchers and academics around the globe. Organisational culture itself is often described as the values that hold an organisation together, yet academics have struggled to find consensus on a precise definition of culture (Frontiera, 2010). However, a depth of organisational culture can be achieved when it becomes embedded in everything the organisation or group does, with values influencing decisions without conscious application (Schein, 2010).

Schein (1992) provides a definition of organisational culture by describing it as a pattern of shared basic assumptions, learning through problem solving related to external adaptation and internal integration. These aspects can be taught to new members of a group as the correct way to perceive, think and feel when entering or integrating into a group. Maitland et al. (2015) assert that previous research regarding organisational culture can be broadly divided into three categories: integration, differentiation and fragmentation, although there is a requirement to clearly define and operationalise organisational culture in order to move towards greater understanding of the complexity of organisations. Moreover, Lussier and Kimball (2019) also identify three components of culture, although they categorise these components as behaviour, values and beliefs, and assumptions.

An overriding agreed definition is problematic to achieve given the diversity in the definitions and outlooks identified here. Indeed, it has been argued that all cultural diagnosis is detached from actual culture, in much the same way that individual behaviour is removed from actual personality (Smith & Shilbury, 2004). What we do know is that organisational culture varies within organisations from strong to weak, and much of the strength of the culture we can observe is dependent upon the engagement and belief demonstrated from the workforce:

> In organizations with strong cultures, people unconsciously share assumptions and consciously know the organization's values and beliefs. That is, they agree with the organization's assumptions, values,

and beliefs and behave as expected. In organizations with weak cultures, many employees don't behave as expected – they don't share underlying assumptions. They question and challenge the beliefs. When people don't agree with the generally accepted values and beliefs, they may rebel and fight the culture. This can be destructive or constructive.

(Lussier & Kimball, 2019, pp. 153–154)

If we return to the work of Schein (1990, 1992), three distinct levels of organisational culture are outlined: namely artefacts, values and underlying assumptions. If we then relate these levels of organisational culture to match officials specifically, we can start to appreciate how match officials might become positively or negatively engaged with the culture of the organisation in which they operate. We know that match officials, and their management and operational environment are unique, both in the wider world of business and management operations, and within sport itself, with some of the challenges that they face classified as distinctive (Webb et al., 2016). The first or outer level of Schein's model involves the artefacts that an organisation makes public. These artefacts can be aspects such as a vision statement or a company slogan and provide indications of the deeper levels of an existent culture. In terms of match officials, the support and vision of the organisation is extremely important in order that they feel valued and supported in their roles. For example, a company slogan could be something such as the Respect Programme in football, and the strapline that is designed to reduce the amount of abuse directed towards match officials.

Values form the second level of culture in Schein's model, and these values are reflected in how members of the group or organisation interact with each other, how they interact within their environment and what traits, such as honesty of integrity, that group members share (Schein, 1992). This is where the role of match officials becomes more difficult to entwine within extant research and organisational theory. Match officials operate within governing bodies and competitions such as leagues, but crucially with other group members, such as players, coaches and spectators, who can all be considered stakeholders in the sport in question, and effect and impact upon their values. Match officials can consider themselves to be virtuous and honest and operating with integrity, but that does not mean that players, spectators and coaches conduct themselves in the same way. It is the behaviour of these other stakeholders which can negatively impact the match official and make their role within the organisation more problematic. These actions also influence the operational environment in which match officials function.

The final level of culture that Schein identifies is the deepest level of organisational culture, which consists of underlying assumptions (Schein,

1992). In functional and healthy organisations underlying assumptions can provide the basis for the values which are identified in the second level of culture; for example, if integrity is valued and considered essential in the fabric of an organisation, the underlying assumption could be that honesty can lead to success and achievement within the organisation. This can be related to the wider behaviour of players, coaches and spectators and the tolerance or acceptance of negative behaviour towards a match official within a governing body or league. If a lead is not taken from those in positions of governance within these organisations, match officials will feel unsupported, disenfranchised and demotivated, ultimately leading to discontinuation which stems from the inability to create a sustainable and manageable culture within their respective organisations.

Organisational culture and intention to leave

Organisational culture itself is a fundamental aspect of the framework of sport in the UK and across the world. Organisational culture can be concentrated around matters related to common management of organisational problems, as well as leadership in sport (Fletcher & Arnold, 2011). Sports organisations are all fundamentally different, although we can also see some common characteristics displayed through the configuration of their structural dimensions. Parent, O'Brien, and Slack (2012) outline how organisational structure more generally can be described in three ways in terms of *complexity* (how differentiated an organisation is); *formalisation* (documentation such as rules, regulations, policies, procedures and job descriptions, all dictating the operational workings of a sporting organisation); and *centralisation* (the level in hierarchy in a particular sporting organisation where the decisions are made).

These factors are crucial in the management of any individuals within sport, such as players or coaches, and the notion of the individual and their relationship with the organisation (Old, 2013). However, given the unique organisation and management related to match officials across all levels of sport, effective organisation and leadership becomes even more essential (Webb et al., 2016). It is true that the values that underlie organisational culture likely reflect what is most important to the leaders of an organisation with previous research demonstrating that organisational culture has played a key role in job satisfaction and increased retention rates among employees (Adkins & Caldwell, 2004; MacIntosh & Doherty, 2005, 2010).

Macintosh and Doherty (2010) found that of the cultural dimensions shown to impact job satisfaction, atmosphere was the most meaningful, with the atmosphere embodying the notion that a workplace that is welcoming, friendly and upbeat will be the most effective. Moreover, the cultural dimension of connectedness had a significant influence on the intention of employees to leave, with perceptions indicating that a sense of family or community helps to promote a sense of belonging and moderately influences the likelihood that they will not discontinue. Creating a working environment that has employees or staff who engage with each other in friendly interaction and exchanges assists in combating retention problems (Macintosh & Doherty, 2010). For sports match officials, it is essential to foster a supportive and inclusive culture to encourage their effective recruitment and retention, with the match official departments at governing bodies responsible for the vision and purpose of the organisation of match officials (Macintosh & Doherty, 2010).

Cole and Martin (2018) focused on the importance of a winning culture within professional sport and the role that organisational theory can play in this relationship. Considering rugby union, Cole and Martin (2018) identified the importance of core values, although they also acknowledged that these can be impacted upon by employees or players who do not buy into the ethos that has been created. Moreover, the importance of culture and the status of culture within an organisation must be reinforced, and is influenced by the leadership styles employed by those in positions of governance, as well as the structure of the organisation, the strategies employed and key components such as consistent values (Cole & Martin, 2018). It is also the case that successful teams or groups of people in sport have shared values, with these often subjective and differing between winning teams or organisations (Buono & Bowditch, 2003; Cotterill, 2013; Hartnell, Yi Ou, & Kinicki, 2011).

The structure of organisations, the systems that are in place and the confidence and ingrained trust in these systems from the workforce, all contribute towards a positive organisational culture. For match officials, this trust can manifest itself in assurance towards the governing body in supporting them, confidence in the disciplinary procedures that are in place and ultimately, security as a part of the overarching support and management systems in place around match officials. Any mistrust or breakdown in the relationship between the governing body and the match officials, particularly when mediating abuse, has the potential to positively or negatively contribute towards the prevalence of abuse. Having discussed the general premises of organisational culture and how this may be applied to match officials, we now draw upon the existing research and data to establish the extent to which match officials have experienced organisational culture across the sports under investigation in this book, and in England particularly in this chapter.

In terms of match officials, importance is placed upon the availability and usefulness of the support around them. Rugby union referees have identified that there should be a programme or campaign to promote respect towards referees, similar to that launched in football in England. As this rugby union referee (male, 6–10 years' experience, 45–54 age group) stated: "We need an effective RESPECT campaign for officials similar to those in junior rugby such as the '#NoRefNoGame' campaign". This is further supported by the fact that some rugby union referees believe that their local or regional society should be providing additional support, in the form of improved, proactive contact instigated through the referee societies. To illustrate, this rugby union referee (male, 3–5 years' experience, 45–54 age group) argued that support should be provided through societies after matches where particular issues have transpired: "The society must provide greater support of referees following matches in which there has been abusive behaviour by requiring clubs to take action subsequently". Another rugby union referee (male, 3–5 years' experience, 45–54 age group) exemplified the feeling that a lack of support from his society means that he has to officiate differently to other referees, implementing strict disciplinary standards prior to the match which players must adhere to: "As there's little support given by the society, I operate a position of zero tolerance under Law 10.4 S which I emphasise in my pre-match briefings".

A particular concern pertinent in rugby union, but a sentiment that can also be applied to other sports, is in regard to recruitment and retention issues of match officials and the attractiveness of a career as a match official. If the culture within this organisational structure is not effective, then it can be difficult to arrest declining match official numbers. The lack of action in terms of changing the status quo is demonstrated by one rugby union referee (male, 11–15 years' experience, 45–54 age group) as one of the principal reasons that he will leave the sport:

> The future of the volunteer 'community rugby referee' looks uninviting. Beyond poster or email reminders to club committees, I see few actions being undertaken to discourage the watchers or participants of this sport from 'the referee is at fault criticisms'. Without doubt it will be the straw that breaks this camel's back – eventually!

The identification of a lack of action by governing bodies is replicated in football. The success, or otherwise, of the Respect Programme (see Chapter 2) is a subject which is often discussed (Wilson, 2016, 2018). The abuse-related issues in football have been an ongoing concern over a concerted period of time (Webb, 2014), and referees have been the recipients of a considerable amount of this abuse, hence the introduction of the Respect Programme in 2008 (Cleland et al., 2015, 2018). However, the implementation of the Respect Programme has drawn negative comments from referees involved in grassroots football. One referee (male, 11–15 years' experience, 55–64 age group) believed that referees at youth and grassroots level are disenfranchised with the FA, stating that there are issues with the communication procedures to referees and to clubs:

> Most refs I know at grassroots level have little faith in the FA achieving the standards set out in 'Respect' and as a consequence are reluctant to report . . . most of us have full time jobs and are unable to take time to attend disciplinary hearings for serious offences. When I have made reports nothing ever seems to get done and certainly never heard about. If you want to make a difference you need to make sure all clubs are aware that action is or has been taken.

The time issue, particularly related to the fact that officiating is a voluntary activity for many match officials, was acknowledged across the data. Moreover, the preceding referee and many others we could have used here identified issues concerning a lack of consistent and transparent action relating to disciplinary reports, communicating that insufficient punishments for the offending clubs or players are evident on most occasions. Indeed, the issues with communication are not unique to football. In cricket, umpires believed that there is some support available from the different competitions that they officiate within, although umpires also stated that the ECB is not often involved in terms of supporting umpires outside the elite level of the game. One umpire (male, 6–10 years' experience, 25–34 age group) discussed the fact that competitions are generally quite supportive of umpires, whereas the ECB is more reliant on guidance that has been developed for dissemination to umpires:

> The competition organisers are usually supportive of their umpires and after investigatory processes are completed, the relevant player/official is banned, fined, or warned as appropriate. The ECB does not directly interfere in supporting umpires or manage incidents of verbal abuse, but it has developed a framework and guidance to demonstrate to participants what is, and what is not, acceptable.

Another umpire also stated that there were issues around the disciplinary process in cricket. The umpire (male, 16–20 years' experience, 45–54 age group) outlined two incidents of both verbal and physical abuse which he had reported, with different outcomes for both incidents: "I reported it and went to a disciplinary hearing (for physical abuse). There was no further action to the player which was disappointing . . . verbal abuse, I reported it to the league and the players were reprimanded/suspended accordingly".

There are clearly discrepancies in the disciplinary procedures to which match officials are beholden in upholding their decisions, judgements and ultimately the laws of the game. Perceived concerns about the disciplinary process and lack of support for match officials evidently lead to the non-reporting of abusive incidents.

Non-reporting: problems in the systems

Working cohesively is imperative when dealing with concerns related to the abuse of match officials in sport. The leaders or those with key roles in governing bodies, leagues or any organisation involved in the management of match officials, need to demonstrate how an organisation will function, and where the culture they have embedded will lead the organisation in question (Schein, 2004). It is also important for match officials, in particular, given that many at lower levels of sport operate in isolation, to have trust in their governing bodies and those involved in the organisation and leadership of match officials. This can be framed as institutional and interpersonal trust, which is often associated with long-term success of organisations (Byers & Thurston, 2016). Given the importance of trust for match officials, the organisation of these individuals at local, regional and national level becomes vitally important. If we consider football, and the structure of the game in England, we can see that referees can receive training, also depending on their level of operation, from the Professional Game Match Officials Limited (PGMOL – who are responsible for the training, development and mentoring of referees who operate predominantly in the professional game), the FA, County FAs, the Referees Association, charities (such as RefSupport) and other localised organisations. The involvement of all of these organisations means that it is difficult to present a unified and cohesive support network to match officials in football.

In local football, match officials operating in local leagues are predominantly organised and managed by the County FAs, who place referees at matches, deal with disciplinary issues and generally facilitate and govern the structure of grassroots football in England. County FAs are responsible for player and club registration and promoting development amongst those clubs, players and referees. This means that clear processes for the reporting, monitoring and intervention of abusive behaviours towards match officials become difficult to organise and govern (Stirling & Kerr, 2008), resonating with the unpredictable reporting and inadequate specification of detail of abusive incidents identified in other sports-related literature (Brackenridge, Bringer, & Bishopp, 2005). Some match officials do not believe they are adequately supported by the system processes and/or those in management roles. As such, they believe that reporting incidents at all is not worthwhile which is indicative of an organisational culture underpinned by a lack of trust in which the non-reporting of abusive incidents is increasingly common and accepted. This is a significant issue for governing bodies and match officials both in terms of tackling matters related to abuse and attempting to identify and track the trends and impact of abuse towards match officials. To further illustrate a lack of cohesiveness and weak organisational culture, one rugby union referee (male, 16–20 years' experience, 45–54 age group) believed that as a strong character, he did not actually need to report incidents and could deal with any issues himself, "I didn't [report the abuse], I am quite a strong person . . . I was happy to take the appropriate action and carded both players and sent spectators back to the club house".

Reference to this strong character in dealing with players will not be evident in all match officials. In cricket, for example, there are concerns in terms of the level of support that some umpires believe they are receiving: "I reported the incident but did not get involved with our Disciplinary Officer's pursuit of the matter. No one tells the truth in these cases . . . the club was also taken to task later in the season for similar behaviour" (Cricket umpire, male, 21+ years' experience, 65+ age group). However, another cricket umpire (male, 11–15 years' experience, 35–44 age group) identified the lack of support from an on-field colleague as a particular issue when considering whether to report the abuse to which they were subjected: "I did not report it as my colleague did not notice the abuse and was not willing to back me up when I suggested reporting". In cases like this, support networks are essential for match officials to operate effectively (Webb, Dicks, Thelwell, van der Kamp, & Rix-Lievre, 2020). If match officials also feel unsupported by their peers and colleagues, this presents a disjointed organisational culture. Match officials are not sure of the value of the reporting process initially, and then unsupported by those that should be their strongest support network – i.e. their colleagues.

This sentiment was also commented upon in football. For example, one referee (male, 21+ years' experience, 55–64 age group) of many from our data believed that verbal abuse can be dealt with more effectively, but that in order to do this other referees must buy into the approach being taken. If some referees decide to take a different attitude, such as dealing with incidents themselves and not reporting the incidents, he argued that it is difficult for any unified approach to work effectively:

> It is possible to eliminate verbal abuse by utilising disciplinary procedures and reporting players/officials/clubs. However, this needs ALL referees to enforce it. There are no real procedures in place to penalise referees who don't, and no feeling of camaraderie, as referees can now simply pass the course and live in their own officiating world. There

is no need to join the referees' society [sic], and, unless they do something wrong and are reported to the County FA it is quite easy to simply turn up and officiate a game, collect the match fee and go home, with little or no commitment to other refereeing colleagues.

The issues presented by match officials across various sports demonstrate a need to repair violations of trust. Because there is a lack of confidence in the support networks and disciplinary procedures, match officials are not reporting a proportion of the incidents to which they are exposed. Trust violations can be due to an individual, team or organisation acting in a way that does not meet the expectations of the match officials (Byers & Thurston, 2016), with competency trust violations seemingly a particular issue in terms of the disciplinary processes in sport (Kim, Dirks, Cooper, & Ferrin, 2006). Further issues arise when match officials begin to take individual ownership of the disciplinary process. This behaviour could be due to the fact that they are not buying into the organisational culture, or the vision, or that the organisational culture or vision itself is not clear. For example, one cricket umpire (male, 11–15 years' experience, 65+ age group) outlined how he approaches disciplinary procedures:

> I have tried not to submit a formal report preferring instead to discuss the matter in a post-match meeting with the captain and player. On the odd occasion when I have submitted a formal report the player has been dealt with appropriately.

Attempting to deal with any incidents of abuse themselves clearly presents safeguarding concerns for the match official in question. This also raises worries around the information not being passed onto the governing bodies, and therefore the governing body in question would not possess all of the information required to either deal with the incident or produce any further action. In football, one referee (male, 16–20 years' experience, 35–44 age group) did not want his actions in dealing with the abuse to impact upon his son who was playing in the match:

> I wish I had reported the abuse. Some of the abuse (parents/managers) was received whilst refereeing my son's games and at times I felt if I had reported the incidents of abuse during these games it may have created problems for my son!

This referee is not alone in believing that they could or should have dealt with a situation differently, and perhaps if it happened again there would be a different action from the referee in question. Another football referee (male, 6–10 years' experience, 45–54 age group) believed that this would also be the case if they were to receive abuse again:

> With verbal abuse it's what's said that matters to me. Some I'm happy to brush off, I may have a word with the player, more often than not though I will caution or send off. I know how emotions can run high and in the heat of the moment things are said. That doesn't make it ok. There is a big difference though between someone who is frustrated to someone who is just simply nasty and a person who has no respect for referees at all. Although I have never suffered physical abuse, I have had a player go for me. I should have sent him off, but he was such a nut case, I really feared for my personal safety and there was only a few minutes of the match remaining. In the end I cautioned him which made me look silly. The other players, especially those on the other team clearly recognised that I had 'bottled it'. I knew this player lived locally and I didn't want to go through the sending off process. I didn't want to be looking over my shoulder when I was out and about. More importantly on the day I just wanted to get home without being attacked. What I do know is that I have thought long and hard about this incident since and I was determined to not let it put me off. I hope that if such an incident was to occur again that I would send the player off and report it.

There are very real safeguarding concerns that are raised with non-reporting, and the reasons that are given for this non-reporting. The first safeguarding concern is around the fact that if teams/players are not reported, it is likely that they will continue to behave aggressively, and therefore other referees or match officials will suffer the same abusive behaviour. The second safeguarding issue is the locality of the match to the place of residence of the referee. There are concerns if referees believe that there are issues with the locality of fixtures that they are assigned, impacting on their home and private lives. Situations such as this have the potential to put referees at risk and if they apply the letter of the law and send certain players off, as they should have done, they risk ongoing concerns over their personal safety.

This culture of non-reporting is also evident in other sports. In rugby league, referees believe that abuse is so ingrained into the culture of the sport that reporting any abusive actions is not worthwhile. As one referee (male, 11–15 years' experience, 35–44 age group) stated: "No, I didn't report it. You just take the vile insults as part of the game". Another referee (male, 21+ years' experience, 35–44 age group), representing many respondents from the data, detailed that the abuse is difficult to manage because it does not always occur on the field of play: "I didn't report the abuse. Verbal abuse tends to be mainly from off-field spectators than anyone on the field". Verbal abuse, in particular, is also subjective and personal in terms of our individual tolerance levels. What one person perceives as verbal abuse, another might not, and this can cause differences in terms of the incidents that match officials are reporting. One football referee (male, 6–10 years' experience, 35–44 age group) explained how this manifests itself in terms of individual tolerance and how young referees can sometimes misinterpret frustration and abuse during a game:

> Whether you feel you have suffered verbal abuse is all dependant on your own tolerance levels. Technically you could argue some form of verbal abuse in every game that you officiate, however it is how you manage it that determines how you feel afterwards. Inexperienced referees especially those that are young and haven't played the game competitively find it hard to distinguish between player frustration and genuine abuse. This also goes back to communication with players etc, which gives you a far greater presence on the pitch.

The individual tolerance and understanding of abuse can impact upon match official communication on the pitch. This perception of abuse can also be extended to how any abuse is reported to the respective governing bodies. Research has been conducted regarding the non-reporting, or "optional reporting" of service complaints by employees (Luria, Gal, & Yagil, 2009). For example, employees have been found to use "avoidance", giving no indication of whether any information was passed to management, and using discretion about whether to report incidents (Luria et al., 2009). Whilst this research is in a different sector, it does provide some grounding for the attitudinal factors around non-reporting. Workers or employees, or in this case match officials, may not want to pass on negative information if they are not sure how those at disciplinary committee level will react or deal with the information that is provided. Moreover, those match officials who want to progress and move up the promotion pathway may be perceived as good match officials, and therefore might view a reporting of an incident of abuse as being seen as a negative character trait or performance issue, as they "want to feel in charge" (Luria et al., 2009).

Despite this, it is important to acknowledge the advancements that are being made in sport. The FA devised and facilitated the Respect Programme in 2008 (see Chapter 2 for further information), and there have been some positive consequences of this programme, such as the inclusion of Respect Marshalls at matches and barriers around the pitch (Webb, Cleland, & O'Gorman, 2017). Rugby league has also attempted to address concerns around abuse (Webb, Rayner, & Thelwell, 2018). However, despite these developments in rugby league, referees believed that they are not as well supported as they should be. One referee (male, 6–10 years' experience, 18–24 age group), for example, believed that the referees require more attention, given the abuse they receive and following the death of Super League referee Chris Leatherbarrow:

> The referee side needs looking into, especially with the amount of abuse and criticism referees come under from spectators and coaches. This has improved a little after the death of Super League referee Chris Leatherbarrow, but improvement is still needed.

It could be argued that the next stage for governing bodies and those in leadership roles is to focus on the care and aftercare of match officials in sport. There is an existing and burgeoning body of research on coaches and their duty to care for players (Cronin, Knowles, & Enright, 2019; Ferguson, Swann, Liddle & Vella, 2019; Kerr & Kerr, 2019), and yet there is very little attention paid to the treatment of match officials by coaches in sport. Moreover, the argument can be made that alongside the duty of care for players, that coaches should also have a duty of care towards match officials. We know that some match officials are discontinuing or are considering discontinuing in a variety of sports, and this will affect the number of competitive sporting fixtures that can be played. We also know that there are a number of reasons that could impact upon match official discontinuation, such as time pressures, family life, perceived lack of support and also abuse (Kellett & Shilbury, 2007; Ridinger, 2015; Webb et al., 2019).

As illustrated in Figure 3.1, when looking across these specific sports,[1] 59.9% of cricket umpires, 37.2% of rugby union referees and 34.4% of rugby league referees either strongly agreed or agreed that episodes of abuse

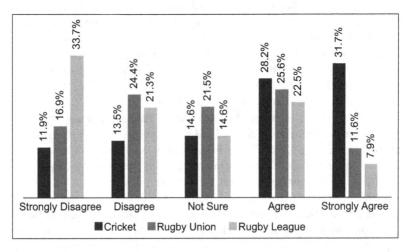

Figure 3.1 Do episodes of abuse make you question whether to continue officiating?

make them question whether to continue officiating. Conversely, 25.4% of cricket umpires, 41.3% of rugby union referees and 55% of rugby league referees either strongly disagreed or disagreed that abusive incidents make them question whether to continue officiating.

Figure 3.2 meanwhile compares whether match officials in cricket, rugby union and rugby league are considering leaving officiating in the next 12 months.

The percentages of match officials who are considering leaving their sport are relatively comparable. Although these numbers are only just higher than 10% of the match official workforce across the sports, if these numbers did decide to discontinue it would make a significant difference to the number of matches and fixtures that could be completed every weekend.

Given these concerns as to whether match officials intend to continue in their sports, it is pertinent to consider why match officials are not reporting incidents and how governing bodies can act in order to change perceptions and therefore increase retention. As we have outlined in this chapter, across sports there is a lack of trust in the disciplinary system that is designed to, at least in part, support match officials in their ability to uphold the laws or rules of the game. We know that not only is trust associated with the long-term success of organisations and their employees, but also that violations in trust through an organisation not acting as expected or a mistrust of competency, such as in the disciplinary process, can lead to discontentment from employees (Byers & Thurston, 2016; Kim et al., 2006). Therefore, the lack of trust in the disciplinary systems across sports is a genuine concern for those in match official governance and leadership roles. By

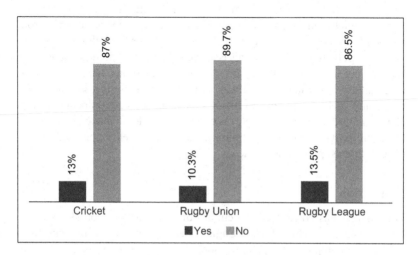

Figure 3.2 Are you thinking of leaving officiating in the next 12 months?

way of illustration, in cricket, the lack of trust in the system is particularly evident in this extract from a cricket umpire (male, 6–10 years' experience, 45–54 age group): "We need a more robust disciplinary procedure where leagues/competition organisers take the initiative in taking action against offenders".

The action taken by governing bodies can provide the feeling of support for match officials, although a lack of action can also have a detrimental impact on the officiating workforce. In English football the concerns revolve around the number of incidents that referees have to deal with during a match and differences in the support at a local and regional level from the County FA and from a national perspective from the FA. One referee (male, 3–5 years' experience, 18–24 age group) highlighted the different support available at regional and national level: "I've reported in some instances where appropriate. Disciplinary action and support from the County FA is good. But the support from the national FA is non-existent". Despite some positive opinions about the County FAs, some referees reported that there were simply too many frequent abusive incidents and therefore reporting them all would be too time-consuming for both the referee and the County FA:

> I have reported a couple of the most serious incidences of verbal abuse, in which cases the full disciplinary proceedings conducted by the county FA were done in a very supportive way, but as stated for the most part abuse is too frequent/minor to make it feasible to report every single incident.
>
> (Football referee, male, 6–10 years' experience, 18–24 age group)

This lack of reporting is concerning for governing bodies. Whether the match official deems a particular act of abuse to be minor or occurring too frequently to report, is not necessarily a decision for the individual match official. A potential remedy for this issue across sports is additional guidance and training for match officials around abusive situations, what constitutes verbal abuse in particular in a given sport and why there is a stipulation to report any such abuse. For governing bodies an accurate reflection of the playing environment in their sport is essential in order to make policy decisions and provide appropriate training and development opportunities for match officials, players and coaches.

Conclusion

This chapter has considered the culture of abuse across football, cricket, rugby union and rugby league in England; actions, in terms of the reporting of abuse; the importance of organisational culture; and consequently how these facets are linked. We have considered the influence that this can have on individual and group behaviour, as well as match officials' perceptions of the management and leadership of abusive incidents. The current landscape across English sport has been considered and the findings demonstrate an environment of abuse, a lack of action from governing bodies, non-reporting of this abuse and a workforce that has some reservations about continuing. Fortunately for those in positions of governance the match official workforces show a commitment to their chosen sport. Despite this, there are still a significant number of match officials who are negatively affected by abuse and are therefore considering whether to continue at all. The level and vociferous nature of the abusive incidents to which match officials are exposed has created issues with recruitment and retention across sports, which is discussed in detail in Chapter 2.

Clearly the reservations of match officials with the disciplinary processes and the support networks mean that many verbal and physical abuse-related incidents are not being reported to the governing bodies. This, in turn, provides the governing bodies of sport an inaccurate reflection of the operational environment for match officials. Whether this is a trust related issue, or whether match officials have become disenfranchised with the environment in which they find themselves, there are visible trends across sports in terms of the perceived support for these match officials. This all points towards a certain apathy from match officials towards local, regional and national governance agencies and feelings of disengagement and isolation from the match official workforces. All of this makes the support networks around match officials and the ability to be resolute and resilient arguably essential traits for sports match officials. Chapter 4 focuses on these support networks, the role of resilience and the importance of conflict management and conflict resolution, particularly given the abuse to which match officials are subjected.

Note

1 Football has not been included in these graphs due to the different formatting of the questions in the football survey.

References

Adkins, G., & Caldwell, D. (2004). Firm or subgroup culture: Where does fitting in matter most. *Journal of Organizational Behavior, 25*(8), 969–978. doi: 10.1002/job.291

Brackenridge, C., Bringer, J. D., & Bishopp, D. (2005). Managing cases of abuse in sport. *Child Abuse Review, 14*, 259–274. doi. 10.1002/car.900

Buono, A., & Bowditch, J. (2003). *The human side of mergers and acquisitions: Managing collisions between people, cultures, and organizations.* San Francisco, CA: Jossey-Bass.

Byers, T., & Thurston, A. (2016). Trust and control in sport organizations. In T. Byers (Ed.), *Contemporary issues in sport management: A critical introduction* (pp. 431–444). London: Sage.

Cleland, J., O'Gorman, J., & Bond, M. (2015). The English football association's respect campaign: The referees' view. *International Journal of Sport, Policy and Politics, 7*(4), 551–563. doi: 10.1080/19406940.2015.1088050

Cleland, J., O'Gorman, J., & Webb, T. (2018). Respect? An investigation into the experience of referees in association football. *International Review for the Sociology of Sport, 53*(8), 960–974. doi: 10.1177/1012690216687979

Cole, J., & Martin, A. J. (2018). Developing a winning sport team culture: Organizational culture in theory and practice. *Sport in Society: Culture, Commerce, Media, Politics, 21*(8), 1204–1222. doi: 10.1080/17430437.2018.1442197

Cotterill, S. (2013). *Team psychology in sports: Theory and practice.* New York: Routledge.

Cronin, C., Knowles, Z. R., & Enright, K. (2019). The challenge to care in a Premier League football club. *Sports Coaching Review.* doi:10.1080/21640629.2019.1578593

Ferguson, H. L., Swann, C., Liddle, S. K., & Vella, S. A. (2019). Investigating youth sports coaches' perceptions of their role in adolescent mental health. *Journal of Applied Sport Psychology, 31*(2), 235–252. doi: 10.1080/10413200.2018.1466839

Fletcher, D., & Arnold, R. (2011). A qualitative study of performance leadership and management in elite sport. *Journal of Applied Sport Psychology, 23*(2), 23–242. doi: 10.1080/10413200.2011.559184

Frontiera, J. (2010). Leadership and organizational culture transformation in professional sport. *Journal of Leadership & Organizational Studies, 17*(1), 71–86. doi: 10.1177/1548051809345253

Hartnell, C. A., Ou, A. Y., & Kinicki, A. (2011). Organizational culture and organizational effectiveness: A meta-analytic investigation of the competing values framework's theoretical suppositions. *Journal of Applied Psychology, 96*(4), 677–694. doi: 10.1037/a0021987

Kellett, P., & Shilbury, D. (2007). Umpire participation: Is abuse really the issue? *Sport Management Review, 10*(3), 209–229. doi: 10.1016/S1441-3523(07)70012-8

Kerr, R., & Kerr, G. (2019). Promoting athlete welfare: A proposal for an international surveillance system. *Sport Management Review, 23*(1), 95–103. doi: 10.1016/j.smr.2019.05.005

Kim, P. H., Dirks, K. T., Cooper, C. D., & Ferrin, D. L. (2006). When more blame is better than less: The implications of internal vs. external attributions for the repair of trust after a competence- vs. integrity-based trust violation. *Organizational Behavior and Human Decision Processes, 99*(1), 49–65. doi: 10.1016/j.obhdp.2005.07.002

Luria, G., Gal, I., & Yagil, D. (2009). Employees' willingness to report service complaints. *Journal of Service Research, 12*(2), 156–174. doi: 10.1177/1094670509344214

Lussier, R. N., & Kimball, D. C. (2019). *Applied sport management skills* (3rd Ed.). Champaign, IL: Human Kinetics.

MacIntosh, E. W., & Doherty, A. (2005). Leader intentions and employee perceptions of organizational culture in a private fitness corporation. *European Sport Management Quarterly, 5*(1), 1–22. doi: 10.1080/16184740500089557

MacIntosh, E. W., & Doherty, A. (2010). The influence of organizational culture on job satisfaction and intention to leave. *Sport Management Review*, *13*, 106–117. doi: 10.1016/j.smr.2009.04.006

Maitland, A., Hills, L. A., & Rhind, D. J. (2015). Organisational culture in sport: A systematic review. *Sport Management Review*, *18*(4), 501–576. doi: 10.1016/j. smr.2014.11.004

Old, J. (2013). Organisational behaviour in sport organisations. In J. Beech & S. Chadwick (Eds.), *The business of sport management* (2nd Ed., pp. 123–147). Harlow: Pearson.

Parent, M., O'Brien, D., & Slack, T. (2012). Organisation theory and sport management. In L. Trenberth & D. Hassan (Eds.), *Managing sport business: An introduction* (pp. 99–120). London: Routledge.

Pettigrew, A. M. (1979). On studying organizational cultures. *Administrative Science Quarterly*, *24*(4), 570–581. doi: 10.2307/2392363

Ridinger, L. (2015). Contributors and constraints to involvement with youth sports officiating. *Journal of Amateur Sport*, *1*(2), 103–127.

Schein, E. H. (1990). Organizational culture. *American Psychologist*, *45*(2), 109–119. doi: 10.1037/0003-066X.45.2.109

Schein, E. H. (1992). *Organizational culture and leadership* (2nd Ed.). San Francisco, CA: Jossey-Bass.

Schein, E. H. (2004). *Organizational culture and leadership* (3rd Ed.). San Francisco, CA: Jossey-Bass.

Schein, E. H. (2010). *Organizational culture and leadership* (4th Ed.). San Francisco, CA: John Wiley & Sons.

Smith, A. C. T., &. Shilbury, D. (2004). Mapping cultural dimensions in Australian sporting organisations. *Sport Management Review*, *7*(2), 133–165. doi: 10.1016/ S1441-3523(04)70048-0

Stirling, A. E., & Kerr, G. A. (2008). Defining and categorizing emotional abuse in sport. *European Journal of Sport Science*, *8*(4), 173–181. doi: 10.1080/ 17461390802086281

Trice, H. M., & Beyer, J. M. (1984). Studying organizational cultures through rites and ceremonials. *Academy of Management Review*, *9*(4), 653–669. doi: 10.5465/ amr.1984.4277391

Webb, T. (2014). The emergence of training and assessment for referees in association football: Moving from the side-lines. *The International Journal of the History of Sport*, *31*(9), 1081–1097. doi: 10.1080/09523367.2014.905545

Webb, T., Cleland, J., & O'Gorman, J. (2017). The distribution of power through a media campaign: The respect programme, referees and violence in association football. *The Journal of Global Sport Management*, *2*(3), 162–181. doi: 10.1080/24704067.2017.1350591

Webb, T., Dicks, M., Thelwell, R., van der Kamp, G. J., & Rix-Lievre, G. (2020). An analysis of soccer referee experiences in France and the Netherlands: Abuse, conflict, and support. *Sport Management Review*, *23*(1), 52–65. doi: 10.1016/j. smr.2019.03.003

Webb, T., Rayner, M., & Thelwell, R. (2018). An explorative case study of referee abuse in English Rugby League. *Journal of Applied Sport Management*, *10*(2). doi: 10.18666/JASM-2017-V10-12-8834

Webb, T., Wagstaff, C. R. D., Rayner, M., & Thelwell, R. (2016). Leading elite association football referees: Challenges in the cross-cultural organization of a geographically dispersed group. *Managing Sport and Leisure, 21*(3), 105–123. doi: 10.1080/23750472.2016.1209978

Wilson, J. (2016). *Exclusive: Referees live in fear as grass-roots game spirals out of control.* Retrieved from www.telegraph.co.uk/football/2016/03/21/exclusive-referees-live-in-fear-as-grass-roots-game-spirals-out/

Wilson, J. (2018). *English football officials seven times more likely to be verbally abused than European counterparts.* Retrieved from www.telegraph.co.uk/football/2018/12/20/english-football-officials-seven-times-likely-verbally-abused/

4 Facilitating a positive environment

The role of resilience, mental fortitude and conflict management when supporting match officials

Introduction

We know from previous research that the abuse of match officials contributes to their discontinuation alongside other factors, such as time and family commitments (Kellett & Warner, 2011; Ridinger, 2015; Ridinger, Kim, Warner, & Tingle, 2017a; Ridinger, Warner, Tingle, & Kim, 2017b; Warner, Tingle, & Kellett, 2013; Webb, Dicks, Thelwell, van der Kamp, & Rix-Lievre, 2020; Webb, Rayner, & Thelwell, 2019). However, we also know the importance of both formal and informal networks of support that exist locally, regionally and nationally, and the prominence that match officials place on these support networks in terms of their development and also, ultimately, their continuation as a match official (Cleland, O'Gorman, & Bond, 2015; Cleland, O'Gorman, & Webb, 2018; Ridinger, 2015; Ridinger et al., 2017a; Webb et al., 2020; Webb et al., 2019).

Previous chapters (see for example Chapter 2 and Chapter 3) have considered the abuse to which match officials are subjected and the importance of the organisational culture that exists within the different governing bodies and support organisations. We also examined the issues that can contribute towards the discontinuation of match officials and the reasons for this discontinuation. This chapter focuses on the importance of the personal and professional support networks that exist around match officials, and the policy initiatives introduced by the four respective sports governing bodies in order to address the concerns over match official abuse impacting on recruitment and discontinuation in England.

Whilst the construction of formal and informal networks is evidently important for match officials in dealing with the challenges they face, resilience is a trait that match officials need to demonstrate in order to operate effectively, progress in their chosen sport or merely survive in the often testing environment in which they operate. This landscape can be charged with stressors for these match officials, making the traits of resilience, mental fortitude and the ability to perform under pressure arguably essential aspects of a match official's personality and performance attributes. However, we know little about the applied importance of resilience and how match officials strive to improve performance under the pressures to which they are exposed. Therefore, the environment, support networks and the personal development opportunities become imperative to understand further if we want to provide positive, facilitative environments that permit match officials to prosper. The chapter considers why match officials may be viewed as an 'outgroup' which legitimises abusive behaviour towards them by players, coaches and spectators and examines solutions to the conflict between the key stakeholders within sport, namely the match officials, players, coaches and spectators.

Consequently, this chapter investigates the essential requirements for effective support networks around match officials to enable them to officiate. We draw upon the findings from extensive survey data to provide headline findings across sports, and subsequently utilise the open response data to examine some of the key issues that emerge. This chapter provides insight intended to be of use to those involved in the management or leadership of match officials across sports and countries, match officials themselves as a method of support and understanding of their community and governing bodies to better understand their match official populations and the challenges that they face. Initially we focus on the role and importance of resilience for match officials, how an understanding of resilience can be utilised for and by English match officials and how this can relate to mental toughness.

The role of resilience for match officials

The ability to demonstrate resilience is arguably an essential trait for match officials, and certainly, those match officials who want to progress through the development pathways in their chosen sport. During the latter years of the 20th and early parts of the 21st century, training programmes have improved for elite match officials. This improvement in training platforms has enabled match officials to increase their resilience in certain situations in which they might find themselves, such as dealing with confrontational players or following an error that they might have made during a fixture (Webb, Dicks, Thelwell, & Nevill, 2018). As a recognition of the importance of the provision of support around elite match officials and linked to improved resilience, a full-time training and development manager and a full-time sports psychologist have been appointed in the English Premier League to assist with some of the concerns identified here (Nevill, Webb, & Watts, 2013; Webb, 2017, 2018). It can be argued that sport is in itself a unique environment in terms of understanding resilience, as participants willingly place themselves into situations that are highly evaluative, with the consequences of winning and losing particularly clear (Galli & Gonzalez, 2015). Initially it is important to understand what we mean when we refer to resilience in sport. Aside from the fact that it is a complex process or trait to be developed, further research is required in order to understand how resilience unfolds over time (Hill, den Hartigh, Meijer, de Jonge, & Van Yperen, 2018). Researchers have considered this phenomenon from a social science (Windle, Bennett, & Noyes, 2011) and psychological perspective (Sarkar & Fletcher, 2014), which focus on why some individuals are able to withstand pressures that they experience in their personal and professional lives. Galli and Gonzalez (2015) emphasise that researchers have taken two primary approaches to dealing with the notion of resilience in sport. First, psychosocial studies tend to concentrate on the prediction of performance following the failure or inadequate performance of an initial task and the resilience demonstrated by the performer in then completing the task in hand successfully (Galli & Gonzalez, 2015). Second, the study of resilience in sport tends to concentrate on understanding the perceptions, thoughts, emotions and behaviours of athletes who have shown propensity for adaptation and successfully overcoming adversity in sport (Galli & Vealey, 2008).

It would be safe to assume that despite the lack of research into the resilience of sports match officials, resilience is a trait or behaviour that match officials require in order to operate effectively. There have been studies which examine the factors that underpin excellence in English Premier League referees (Slack, Maynard, Butt, & Olusoga, 2013), with the important emergent themes identified as mental toughness attributes, opportunities to thrive and effective support networks amongst other things. Nonetheless, previous research has primarily focused on the performance of match officials in a variety of sports, such as officiating excellence in rugby union (Mascarenhas, Collins, & Mortimer, 2005), factors impacting upon excellence in football refereeing (Mascarenhas, O'Hare, & Plessner, 2006) and the relationship between previous motor and visual experience and current officiating experience of expert judges and referees from an embodied cognition stance (Pizzera & Raab, 2012), rather than a resilience perspective.

When related specifically to sports match officials, the concept of resilience can draw upon research from other associated fields and populations to inform and develop thinking in this subject area. Webb and Hill (2020) focused on the management of the stressors and demands placed upon football match officials, and how these match officials can strive to improve performance under pressure. Webb and Hill (2020) argue that match official organisations should provide infrastructures, procedures and frameworks to promote facilitative and supportive environments for their match officials. Any increased support would consequently provide referees with the appropriate environment to improve training and performance through the development of reactive resilience. Also identified as an area of worthy investigation was the importance and benefit for match officials of mental fortitude (Webb & Hill, 2020).

Mental fortitude and toughness in sports match officials

Research demonstrates that a positive and supportive environment is essential for match officials (Fletcher & Sarkar, 2016), as is consideration around how this support can best facilitate success. This can be explained through mental fortitude training programmes, leading to sustained success (see Figure 4.1).

Mental fortitude training programmes identify three factors that contribute to sustained success: a facilitative environment, personal attributes and a challenge mentality. A principal aim of mental fortitude training is to optimise an individual's personal qualities or attributes, so that they are able to withstand the stressors that they encounter. However, these personal qualities can be profoundly affected by other aspects, such as environmental factors

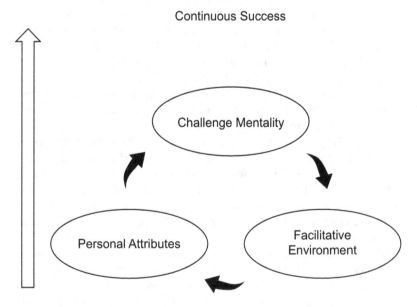

Figure 4.1 Mental fortitude training program for sustained success
Source: (Adapted from Fletcher & Sarkar, 2016).

originating from social, cultural, organisational, political, economic, occupational and/or technological sources (Fletcher & Sarkar, 2016). For match officials, all of these environmental sources can potentially impact upon their participation and effective performances. Moreover, performance levels can increase with greater support provided within the sport-specific environment and for resilience to be developed for sustained success, a facilitative environment should be created and maintained (Fletcher & Sarkar, 2016).

The mind-set of the individual match official is also important when considering mental fortitude and sustained success. Indeed, perhaps the most central or fundamental facet of any resilience training programme is for individual match officials to positively evaluate any pressure they confront, together with their own resources, thoughts and emotions (Fletcher & Sarkar, 2012). It is important to emphasise that resilience is not a weakness and should not be seen as such. In fact, evidence tells us that both resilience and vulnerability co-exist in everybody and it is possible for any individual to suffer extreme adversity and hardship (Fletcher & Sarkar, 2016).

In addition, we can consider the importance of environmental characteristics for match officials, which affect and impact resilience. These characteristics can be grouped into stagnant environments, unrelenting environments, conformable environments and facilitative environments (Fletcher & Sarkar, 2016). For example, in a stagnant environment issues for match officials would manifest themselves around a lack of leadership, a lack of stimulation for match officials, mediocrity, a lack of motivation and performance outcomes being achieved by accident rather than by design. Conversely, at the other end of the spectrum we can see a facilitative environment which includes support to challenge match officials towards a goal, individuals taking ownership of their goals, good relationships between match officials and those in leadership or coach roles with individuals supporting each other and people learning from mistakes together with an inclusive attitude (see Figure 4.2).

Across our data, match officials identified the need for strong support networks around them to facilitate their performances and to ensure their retention in their chosen sport. For example, the majority of cricket umpires identified the support provided as poor, but more importantly, that this poor support system was an accepted part of the game. As expressed by this cricket umpire (male, 6–10 years' experience, 55–64 age group): "The support network for the panel I umpire in is poor, but everyone just seems to accept it. More support equals better development". By way of exemplification, another cricket umpire (female, 21+ years' experience, 65+ age group) suggested that leagues need to demonstrate greater support for umpires and the disciplinary hearings require further thought in terms of their structure and organisation: "We need stronger support from league committees when complaints are made concerning adverse behaviour of players. (Because of

Stagnant Environment	Unrelenting Environment	Comfortable Environment	Facilitative Environment
■ Unseen leaders and managers ■ People are not stimulated ■ People are just going through the motions ■ Culture of mediocrity ■ Little going on ■ Good performance by accident more than by design ■ People don't know what to do or don't care	■ Unhealthy competition ■ Leader exposes / ridicules underperformers ■ Blame culture if high standards not met ■ Little care for wellbeing ■ People feel isolated ■ Potential conflict ■ Performance is not sustainable ■ Stress / potential burnout ■ "Sink or swim"	■ Over-caring, parent like culture ■ People are "nice" ■ Too cosy ■ People working in their comfort zones ■ People are bored ■ Ambiguity and uncertainty ■ Stifling for individuals wanting to be stretched ■ Difficult conversations avoided ■ Lack of personal / professional development ■ Lack of celebration of achievement ■ Underperformance not addresses ■ "A happy performer will be a great performer"	■ Supportive challenge towards a goal ■ People thrive in a challenging but supportive environment ■ Individuals have input into and take ownership of goals ■ Individuals seek out challenges to develop ■ Individuals crave constructive feedback ■ Good relationships between performers and leaders / coaches ■ Psychologically safe environment that encourages sensible risk-taking ■ Healthy competition ■ Everyone supporting one another ■ Learn from mistakes / failures ■ Success recognised and celebrated ■ "We're in this together"

Figure 4.2 Environment characteristics affecting resilience

Source: (Adapted from Fletcher & Sarkar, 2016).

the topography of my county, disciplinary hearings are hard to arrange but need to be within a couple of weeks of an incident)".

Rugby union referees meanwhile also identified support networks as a concern in terms of their performance. In particular, rugby union referees commented on how the communication that they receive is not considered acceptable. For example, this rugby union referee (male, 6–10 years' experience, 45–54 age group) explained how meetings were considered too irregular: "There is very poor communication, monthly meetings are basic at best, finding out about courses, kit, rule changes etc is not easy and observers contradict each other". Despite the concerns raised about communication by some rugby union referees, there are positive aspects of the training. This is predominantly provided through societies, although as with other sports the service delivered by the societies tends to differ depending on location and personnel. By way of illustration, this referee (male, 21+ years' experience, 65+ age group) discussed how the society-run classes operate, and how they have impacted upon his refereeing:

The Society runs monthly classes on refereeing topics which are extremely helpful. They are open to all grades covering all topics giving advice on the different aspects of refereeing including positioning, control and law interpretation. They build confidence which the Advisors also seek to achieve. These classes have certainly helped me improve and changed my style after 20 years of refereeing. I only wish they had been running when I started.

The introduction of the classes by societies appears to have been well received, with a noticeable difference in training and development over the past 20 years, a sentiment supported by other referees, although there was also the understanding that rugby union has changed, in terms of the speed of the game and the pressure on referees, with the support required considered greater. This was illustrated by one rugby union referee (male, 21+ years' experience, 65+ age group) who outlined: "The new referee is given far more support than in my day. Having said that, the pressures in today's games are far greater and a new referee needs every support he/she can get to survive the initial games". There still appears to be variability between the training and support provided from societies, and this variability between the societies is demonstrated through the development pathways that serve to promote and support referees, as illustrated by this rugby union referee (female, 3–5 years' experience, 18–24 age group):

> There could be some standardisation in the development framework used by societies, right from the bottom levels. I have been a member of several societies, and whilst in theory all referees are assessed against the same criteria, each society seems to value different qualities in their referees and promote against different values. Equally, I think if possible, there should be more standardised assessor training at a lower level, so that all referees get some consistency in their feedback.

Similar concerns and issues were raised by rugby league referees who identified a lack of effective communication and felt that regular contact with experienced referees would help in the development of those who are younger and less experienced. To illustrate this, one referee (male, 3–5 years' experience, 35–44 age group) representing a consensus from the wider dataset, believed that communication and also training and development required further thought throughout the game: "We need communication at all levels. We need experienced grade 1 or former grade 1 referees allocated to you as a first port of call to discuss parts of your game to help improve". In addition to this support, referees believed that they need more feedback from their matches, and this would also involve increased numbers of referees or assessors in order to provide the feedback that they require. This rugby league referee (male, 2 years or less experience, 25–34 age group) reiterated the importance of feedback from assessors, but also understood the pressures associated with the provision of assessors: "More feedback from games, so basically more assessors made available. I understand it is voluntary for many of them, but we need to find a way of getting more people involved in rugby league". The voluntary nature of the support network is something that referees cannot control, and it would potentially take a change in culture for more referees to give their time voluntarily. This is a challenge which would prove difficult with declining match official numbers.

Furthermore, rugby league referees identified that in order for support to be improved at lower levels, the RFL as the governing body should assist local organisations such as leagues, and referee societies to encourage referees to attend meetings and embolden more voluntary contributions from experienced referees. One referee (male, 11–15 years' experience, 35–44 age group) believed that it is the role of the RFL to offer this support to societies, and to be more forceful in their guidance about attending meetings: "The RFL need to help society's more, and the RFL need to insist that senior referees should be members of their local society, and to attend meetings". Despite the concerns evidenced around the training provided and the uptake of the training opportunities, as we outline in Figure 4.3, match officials from football, cricket, rugby union and rugby league in England believed that the training was valuable.

Across rugby union, rugby league and cricket, match officials present some differences regarding their perceptions of the training products offered by the different governing bodies. Despite some level of contentment evident, there are variances between the sports. For example, 70.8% of cricket umpires thought the training products were either very good or good, whereas 28.1% of rugby league referees believed that the training products were either very good or good. However, 37.1% of rugby league referees also believed that the training products were poor or very poor.

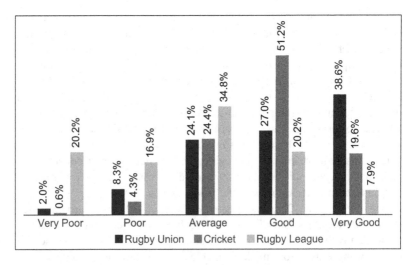

Figure 4.3 What is your view of the current training products offered?*

* Rugby union respondents were asked to consider training products offered by the RFU, cricket respondents by the ECB and rugby league respondents by the RFL

Match officials were also asked their views regarding the personal development opportunities that they were offered (see Figure 4.4), again evidencing some differences between the sports.

The perception of the development opportunities and the support provided through this training and development* are important for match officials. The opportunities provided also help match officials to belong to a community, with a positive and supportive environment essential for match officials to develop and to contribute to their retention in their chosen sport (Fletcher & Sarkar, 2016). There are differences evident in the responses between the sports. For example, 68% of rugby union referees believed that the development opportunities provided to them by the RFU were either very good or good, whereas 50.4% of cricket umpires and 44.9% of rugby league referees identified that the development opportunities provided by the governing bodies were either very good or good. There are also match officials who believed that the development opportunities required attention, with 18% of rugby league referees, 14.8% of cricket umpires and 9.8% of rugby union referees stating that the development opportunities were either very poor or poor.

The support offered by governing bodies, regional governance organisations, local match official associations and other groups becomes essential to recruit and retain match officials in sport. Without the feeling of support

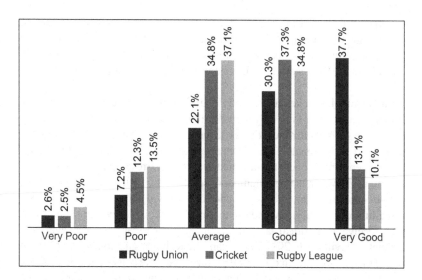

Figure 4.4 What is your view of the current personal development opportunities offered to match officials?*

* Rugby union respondents were asked to consider development opportunities offered by the RFU, cricket respondents by the ECB and rugby league respondents by the RFL

and the requisite training match officials can feel isolated and become identified as an 'outgroup' in sport (Webb et al., 2019, 2020).

In cricket, at the sub-elite level umpires identified that they often stand
alone and that this creates a feeling of pressure for those umpires. For
example, one umpire (male, 2 years' experience or less, 55–64 age group)
explained how operating individually can be a negative experience: "Unfortunately most of my assignments as an umpire, I have been standing alone.
This being the case I am under pressure for every delivery and decision. The
need is for more officials to help relieve pressure". Other cricket umpires
believed that the best way to deal with this isolation and pressure was to
increase the amount of off-field support for both umpires and players. This
off-field support for players should focus on educating them, so that there
is an improvement to the environment, as explained by this umpire (male,
6–10 years' experience, 55–64 age group): "We need off field support to
look to educate players about the umpires' role and help to create less confrontation around decisions on the field".

Rugby union referees also agreed that support was crucial, although
some identified that pressure was an added issue, similar to cricket umpires,
with the first couple of matches for new referees believed to be a particular
concern. This rugby union referee (female, 3–5 years' experience, 25–34
age group) reflected the thoughts of some referees on this topic:

> being able to speak to the society about it, receive advice on how to
> handle the situation in future should it occur. As a new referee this was
> important. The society spoke to the club and also made comments at a
> clubs' meeting stating such actions aren't tolerated by the society.

Clearly, initial matches for recently qualified match officials are extremely
important in terms of not only their development, but also whether they even
stay in the sport at all. A negative experience can lead to a feeling of disenfran-
chisement and ultimately discontinuation, as previously discussed in Chapter 3. Therefore, support for new match officials, irrespective of the sport, is
essential. However, across a number of sports, match officials were asking for
greater support and more training and for localised and regional governance
to be improved. Indeed, we know that match officials view the support that
they receive as a critical factor in achieving success at whatever level they
officiate (Nevill et al., 2013). For example, Ridinger and colleagues (2017b)
found that 20% of match officials they surveyed were considering discontinuing due to a lack of support from administrative authorities. In our data, the
responses of rugby league referees resonated with this interpretation, with
one referee (male, 11–15 years' experience, 25–34 age group) reflecting the
thoughts of many other referees, arguing: "More structured support directly

from the RFL to help local societies" was required. Evidently, not only is there concern that societies in rugby league are not providing the services that match officials feel they should, but also that the societies themselves are not adequately supported by the RFL to achieve this.

This sentiment is echoed by the match official respondents in rugby union. Referee societies were identified as providing a lack of support, particularly concerning the disciplinary process. For example, this rugby union referee (male, 3–5 years' experience, 45–54 age group), reflecting the views of many others, identified the importance of support for referees who have been subjected to an abusive incident: "The society must provide greater support for referees following matches in which there has been abusive behaviour by requiring clubs to take action". Another referee (female, 3–5 years' experience, 25–34 age group) commented that the attitude of the societies would be helped by having a more welcoming and approachable outlook: "Continual conversations and an 'open door' policy with all members of the society". Moreover, rugby union referees commented that despite the training that is on offer from referee societies and the RFU, more could be made available to match officials in terms of training and specific directives related to the interpretation of law. Specifically, it is the communication of these matters which referees believed required greater clarity as explained by this rugby union referee (6–10 years' experience, 35–44 age group):

> I am well aware of what is on offer to help with training, but the material could be made more widely available using the internet and the RFU website. In addition, it would help if refereeing directives were published on the RFU website as well as being emailed to Societies. The email cascade down approach for information on refereeing and law changes doesn't always catch everyone and should be augmented with the RFU and indeed the World Rugby websites.

Football referees also identified the need for greater support, with communication a particular concern. This communication can be addressed through increased inclusion of referees in football, something which football referees believed was a worry. One referee (male, 6–10 years' experience, 35–44 age group), by way of illustration, explained how this support can be provided: "There needs to be greater inclusion of all referees . . . there needs to be follow up training for all referees to understand the laws of the game". Similar to the issues related to the laws of the game in rugby union, football referees who responded to the survey also believed that further training was required in relation to the laws of the game. The wider issue of communication was a matter raised by football referees, although the disciplinary process was also considered a particular concern, as this referee, among many examples we could have selected, identifies here:

> There is still a need for more support to referees from the FA County disciplinary committees. It is often quite difficult, several weeks later, at these committees to get to the real reason for disrespect at any point in the game but better communication from the FA to the referee after the hearing would help feelings of discontent.

(Football referee, male, 21+ years' experience, 55–64 age group)

The fact that there is discontent is a concern in terms of wider governance. Moreover, this discontent is evident due to a requirement of additional support for match officials in football, particularly at County FA level, a sentiment which was also described by another referee (male, 21+ years' experience, 55–64 age group):

> Referees need the full support of the relevant County Football Association . . . the fines for players/club officials MUST be increased to a realistic level. The FA should keep a separate pot of money from the top level to help grass roots football.

Clearly, match officials across sports believed that greater support was required in order for them to fulfil their roles as effectively as possible. The support of the national governing bodies is essential, as is the support of regional governing bodies, both identified as a vital piece of the support structure. This finding is particularly concerning given that effective support and interaction with governing bodies are considered imperative to retain referees in sport (Kellett & Warner, 2011; Warner et al., 2013).

Furthermore, the identification of an increase in fines for players and clubs who are disrespectful towards match officials is designed to dissuade abuse towards match officials with the English FA advised to separate the income from these fines to assist with the support for referees in grassroots football. It is this support that match officials believed required further consideration. However, it is also evident from extant research that it is difficult to resolve due to the way that match officials are perceived within sport, with these match officials identified as a separate 'outgroup' with different aims and objectives than those of the players, coaches and spectators.

Intergroup conflict and conflict resolution

The notion of intergroup conflict can be employed to resolve some of the issues which have been identified in this book. Match officials can be considered as an 'outgroup' within the sport that they officiate, they are not concerned with who will win or lose, they are concerned with upholding the laws of the game and ensuring that decisions are made fairly, in order to allow the teams to participate and play to the same set of laws and standards. Previous research has identified that football referees in particular have to deal with specific concerns related to abusive behaviour from players, coaches and spectators (Webb et al., 2020). Conflict between groups is also not uncommon in wider society (McDonald, Navarrete, & Van Vugt, 2012). These conflicts can be on a larger scale, such as a diplomatic issue that has escalated between two countries, or the conflict can be on a smaller scale, can often involve competition, aggression and/or antipathy, and can intensify following disagreements and percep-tions of injustice (Bornstein, 2003; McDonald et al., 2012). These instances of antipathy and injustice can be amplified when individuals are part of a larger group, with shared aims and objectives, and as such, we can start to comprehend the divergent objectives of each of the groups within sport. For example, we can consider match officials as a distinct 'group' within sport, and as such players, coaches and spectators can be classified as another 'group', then the differences in the objectives of these groups can lead to an inflated adverse reaction towards the 'outgroup' – i.e. match officials (Böhm, Rusch, & Baron, 2018; Branscombe & Wann, 1992; Jackson, 2002).

As a result of this understanding, we can further consider the role that intergroup conflict plays, which can mean that players, spectators and coaches might engage in conflict that results in substantial negative con-sequences for the outgroup members, or match officials in this context (Mäs & Dijkstra, 2014). Reducing differences between the ingroup (players, coaches and spectators) and the outgroup (match officials) becomes essen-tial in order to challenge issues between the groups. Research has shown that positive intergroup contact can be associated with reduced prejudice towards an outgroup, with positive interactions with members of the out-group contributing to changes in these relationships, such as when a group's physical safety is threatened. In the case of decreased physical safety, fear is likely to be stirred, especially when the group, or match officials, feel powerless (Christ et al., 2014; Kamans, Otten, & Gordijn, 2010).

In terms of sport-specific research related to intergroup conflict, Weisel and Böhm (2015) studied the motivations underlying individual participa-tion in intergroup conflict between natural groups, incorporating supporters of football clubs. The findings identified that increased understanding of intergroup conflict is linked to an improved comprehension of the individ-ual motivation for participation in any particular conflict, and that any such conflict depends on the amount of hostility between the groups involved. To illustrate this, we now provide a case study scenario taken from a real incident in cricket, which was reported in the 2019 season, as evidence of the conflict to which sports match officials are exposed.

Case study – umpire abuse incident report, local cricket match 2019

The case study outlined in the following is taken from a report of an incident in local league cricket in England. This report is the testament provided to the league disciplinary committee by the umpire. Any team names have been removed and the umpire and player names have been changed to maintain anonymity.

Pre-amble

As the Spartan players started to arrive, I welcomed their players and pointed them towards the changing room. A Spartan player pointed me towards their captain, Mr Smith. I went towards him and introduced myself as the Trojans captain. He informed me that he would "speak to me when he was ready mate". I thought this was a little unfriendly but left him to go the changing rooms. At 1.15pm he requested we complete the toss as he had "places to be after the match". The toss was won by Trojans. I elected to bowl to which he commented "really". I also informed him I was still waiting for two players and after phoning them was expecting them to arrive after 1.30pm. He commented that if they did not arrive by 1.30pm he would consider "reversing the toss". I told him that I would start with 9 players. I informed the Spartan's umpires and scorers of this and they consented to allow the two remaining players to enter the field of play when they arrived. They subsequently did allow this.

Given the less than friendly tone of the Spartan captain I briefed my team on my experience before the match started. In my view the Spartan captain had already breached the spirit of cricket pre-amble but with junior cricket we accept that, assuming they are aware of it, each club and individual player may interpret the pre-amble in a different way.

Bar the very first ball when Trojans appealed loudly for an LBW (the ball having hit the batsman on the toe of the boot) in my view, the Spartan's innings was played in a fair manner. I discussed this batsman's (Mr Johnson) subsequent dismissal (he left the field in a very unsportsmanlike manner) with the Spartan's square leg umpire (Mr Bailey) and assured him that our intention as a team is the play in a fair and honest manner. Mr Bailey agreed with this and did not believe we had done anything unfair in the dismissal of Mr Johnson. We both discussed having attended umpiring courses and passing the initial examination.

The incident

I was standing umpire for the third over. I called a front foot no ball. The Spartan's captain was fielding in the slips and made the following audible comment, "Don't worry mate (to the bowler) he hasn't a fucking clue (directed at me as the umpire) he is just trying to get in your f****g head". Later in the over, the bowler bowled a wide ball which I let pass in attempt to defuse the tension. The bowler thanked me for this patting me on the shoulder.

At the start of the fifth over there was an appeal for LBW which as standing umpire I declined and called not out. The response to which was much swearing from the slips where the Spartan's captain and Mr Smith were fielding. The Trojan's batsman turned away from the slip cordon. Mr Smith then attempted a run out which was declined by both me and the square leg umpire, Mr Brocks. The reaction of Mr Smith was to run around in circles screaming, "You f****g cheat", on a number of occasions. At which point I stepped forward past the stumps indicating play should cease under law 41.2.1.

The Spartan's captain then left his fielding position and marched towards Mr Brocks also shouting, "You f*****g cheat" in a loud and intimidatory manner. He continued to do this within inches of Mr Brocks for a number of minutes. By this time, I had left my position as standing umpire and joined Mr Brocks and the Spartans captain with the intention of speaking to the Spartans captain to try and defuse the situation.

Mr Trainer continued to abuse Mr Brocks in a loud and aggressive manner and at no time moderated his language or body posture. Having assessed there was little chance of having a reasoned conversation with Mr Trainer, and believing he had contravened law 41.1 and 42.1.1., Mr Brocks and I withdrew to discuss what we should do.

As the law states under 42.1 matters should be reported to the captain (and Spartans not having made me aware they had a vice captain) I was presented with a dilemma. With the captain

(Mr Trainer) the main culprit, aided and abated by Mr Smith, both Mr Brocks and I felt there was no chance of Mr Trainer calming down or accepting any form of sanction under law 42.1.1. For the safety of my batsman and the remaining team members we decided to withdraw from the field of play. I informed Mr Trainer of this and he responded, "F****g hell mate". There was no subsequent interaction between me and Mr Trainer, and he made no attempt to apologise. The Spartans team then went and sat in a number of groups.

One of these groups subsequently spoke to me. I apologised for the match being abandoned, unprompted they told me that this was not the first time that they had seen this sort of behaviour from Mr Trainer and that I had followed a sensible course of action.

I am somewhat concerned that a significant minority of the Spartans players are aware of the behavioural/temper issues displayed by Mr Trainer on Saturday, yet the club still sees fit to allow him to hold the position of captain. I can only assume that if anybody questions him, they fear risking losing their place in the team.

Post-script

I believe that in holding the position of captain, Mr Trainer has contravened both the spirit of cricket and a number of laws. This may be wilful, or through ignorance. The former needs to be sanctioned, the later should have been dealt with before Spartans cricket club allow him to take the field as captain in future.

Whilst we all put up with petty cheating and ill-informed decisions each Saturday in junior cricket, stepping on to a cricket pitch or any sporting arena, does not convey the right to abuse the opposition verbally, or heaven forbid physically. Nobody wants to spend their Saturdays being sworn at on a repeat basis, intimidated in the name of "playing hard" and bullied in to making incorrect umpiring decisions to avoid controversy. This is not an environment to develop and foster the game that we hear so much about from county boards and the ECB. Club chairs should take responsibility for ensuring cricket is played in a fair and hard manner (as per the ECB) and only appoint captains who are willing to lead by example and follow this mantra.

If the Spartan's board were aware of Mr Trainers' previous behaviour, which a number of players appear to be, then they should also be providing an explanation as to why he is deemed fit and proper to be captain. If they are not aware, I have to question their oversight. Players like Mr Trainer and Mr Smith are leading to the on-going falling participation levels in junior cricket. County boards, Clubs and senior players need to lead by example, creating a positive environment for the game, not one of intimidation and fear as we unfortunately experienced on Saturday. I suspect other clubs have experienced this in the past.

Through the case study and the literature which we have already examined, we can see evidence of the link between the sporting world and social identification through negative feelings towards match officials as an outgroup, and feelings of anger by players, coaches and spectators as an ingroup. The preceding case study evidences the disruptive and abusive behaviour to which the umpires were subjected, and can be linked to work concerning abuse towards match officials that has considered the extent (Ridinger et al., 2017b; Webb et al., 2017) of the abuse, potential methods of tackling abuse and other reasons for discontinuation (Ridinger et al., 2017a). However, the nature of the conflicts between match officials as one group, and players, coaches and spectators as another group necessitates resolutions and inevitably, an improvement to the abusive situations to which match officials have been exposed over time (Webb, 2014, 2016).

If a match official is subjected to a negative experience, the support network around that individual becomes more important. If we take the example of an altercation that leads to an abusive incident, the response from those in governance roles becomes significant, as does the reaction of the individual. The intergroup conflict that exists across sports creates ingroups and outgroups as we have discussed, or an 'us' and 'them' culture, with players, coaches and spectators. Governing bodies should move towards a reduction or removal of this cultural barrier in order to reduce negative reactions towards match officials, create an enhanced working environment and in time, facilitate further growth in the numbers of match officials, as greater numbers register and are retained in their chosen sport.

However, the existence of intergroup conflict requires proactive coping and emotion-focused coping as an effective individual response to interpersonal conflict, as we illustrate in Table 4.1 (Hill, Matthews, & Senior, 2016). To elaborate, abusive behaviour towards a match official can be managed through preparation and a more individualised emotion-focused coping strategy involving relaxation, centring or distancing from the incident itself. Of course, if this is an incident which cannot be dealt with effectively

Table 4.1 Characteristics of performance under pressure (adapted from Hill et al., 2016)

Stressor/Demand	Effective Coping Response	Details
Unfamiliarity	Proactive-coping Informational social support	Prepare for unexpected / best-case / worse-case scenarios before the game, through imagery and accessing expert advice form significant others.
Performance Errors	Acceptance Ownership Reflective practice	Own (rather than deny) the error and use reflective practice (with a significant other) to constructively consider and address the reasons for the mistake. Use (mindfulness) acceptance during / after the game (re: the error).
Interpersonal Conflict	Proactive-coping Emotion-focused coping	Manage abuse / threatening behaviour through preparation (imagine worst-case-scenario and rehearse effective personal response) and individualised emotional- focused coping strategy (e.g. relaxation, centring, distancing). Note specifically, the importance of emotional contagion (the player / crowd responding to [i.e., 'catching'] the referee's emotions) in a hostile context.
Important Game / Moment	Proactive-coping Emotion-focused Task / process-focus	Manage important games by preparing best- / worst-case in advance (see preceding) and use individually tailored behavioural coping strategies to modify emotional state. Utilise process goals to remain focused on task relevant performance information under high levels of pressure.
Scrutiny	Task / process-focus	Adopt process goals to remain focused on task, when under high levels of pressure.

in this way, this might be an ongoing wellbeing or mental health concern, a concept explored further in Chapter 5, alongside the importance of strong policy and governance when supporting match officials.

Conclusion

This chapter has considered the importance of a support network for match officials in England across football, cricket, rugby union and rugby league. Moreover, the role of resilience, the importance of mental fortitude in abusive or challenging situations, the role of intergroup conflict and conflict resolution, as well as effective coping strategies that might be employed by match officials have been discussed. The role of resilience was identified as particularly important for individual match officials. The mind-set of the individual match official is extremely important for their sustained success, which might be continuous development and progression in the development framework of the sport in question, or it might simply be continuing in the sport, content with the environment in which they operate.

In order for discontinuation to be avoided facilitative environments in sports have to be provided (Fletcher & Sarkar, 2016). Positive environments can contribute to continued participation and effective performance, although if these environments are negative or stagnant environments, we can begin to recognise concerns around leadership and a lack of motivation amongst other things (Fletcher & Sarkar, 2016). The findings across the four sports in England identified support systems that require attention if they are to operate more effectively for match officials. The issues identified were varied; however, common trends were described across the sports such as non-existent or poor communication, a lack of governing body support for local match official societies and concerns surrounding match officials feeling isolated when officiating, particularly at lower levels of sport. This is particularly concerning given that this increased support has been determined as essential, given the increasing pressures in the modern game and when considering the fact that 20% of match officials have considered discontinuing principally due to a lack of support from administrative authorities (Ridinger et al., 2017b).

There were some positive observations from match officials, particularly related to improved training and development opportunities. Rugby union referees, for example, believed that support for training had improved significantly in recent years, although this was believed to be in response to the increased pressures faced by match officials rather than addressing or dealing with abusive incidents in the modern game. Acts of abuse directed towards match officials by players, coaches and spectators require stronger support, and the subsequent disciplinary procedures become critical, both in retaining match officials and in providing a duty of care. However, across the sports match officials were concerned with the efficacy of disciplinary procedures. Indeed, match officials across all sports that were surveyed believed that improved communication and more effective support from societies and regional governing bodies is required to prevent feelings of discontent with the procedures and system more widely.

Intergroup conflict and conflict resolution were other areas examined in this chapter, with match officials considered an 'outgroup' within the sport that they officiate. The reaction of players, coaches and spectators towards match officials as the 'outgroup' can be negative, particularly during a competitive fixture (Böhm et al., 2018; Jackson, 2002), and as such mediation, targeted initiatives and a shared purpose amongst these groups are required. In light of some of the issues highlighted during this chapter and in order to address this further, Chapter 5 focuses on the importance of policy and strong governance, and the requirement for good understanding of mental health literacy and wellbeing amongst match officials, particularly given the situations in which they can find themselves during a match.

References

Böhm, R., Rusch, H., & Baron, J. (2018). The psychology of intergroup conflict: A review of theories and measures. *Journal of Economic Behavior & Organization*. doi: 10.1016/j.jebo.2018.01.020

Bornstein, G. (2003). Intergroup conflict: Individual, group, and collective interests. *Personality and Social Psychology Review*, 7(2), 129–145. doi: 10.1207/S15327957PSPR0702_129-145

Branscombe, N. R., & Wann, D. L. (1992). Role of identification with a group, arousal, categorization processes, and self-esteem in sports spectator aggression. *Human Relations*, 45(10), 1013–1033. doi: 10.1177/001872679204501001

Christ, O., Schmid, K., Lolliot, S., Swart, H., Stolle, D., Tausch, N., et al. (2014). Contextual effect of positive intergroup contact on outgroup prejudice. *PNAS*, 111(11), 3996–4000. doi: 10.1073/pnas.1605115113

Cleland, J., O'Gorman, J., & Bond, M. (2015). The English football association's respect campaign: The referees' view. *International Journal of Sport, Policy and Politics*, 7(4), 551–563. doi: 10.1080/19406940.2015.1088050

Cleland, J., O'Gorman, J., & Webb, T. (2018). Respect? An investigation into the experience of referees in association football. *International Review for the Sociology of Sport*, 53(8), 960–974. doi: 10.1177/1012690216687979

Fletcher, D., & Sarkar, M. (2012). A grounded theory of psychological resilience in Olympic champions. *Psychology of Sport and Exercise*, 13(5), 669–678. doi: 10.1016/j.psychsport.2012.04.007

Fletcher, D., & Sarkar, M. (2016). Mental fortitude training: An evidence-based approach to developing psychological resilience for sustained success. *Journal of Sport Psychology in Action*, 7(3), 135–157. doi: 10.1080/21520704.2016.1255496

Galli, N., & Gonzalez, S. P. (2015). Psychological resilience in sport: A review of the literature and implications for research and practice. *International Journal of Sport and Exercise Psychology, 13*(3), 243–257. doi: 10.1080/1612197X.2014.946947

Galli, N., & Vealey, R. S. (2008). "Bouncing back" from adversity: Athletes' experiences of resilience. *Sport Psychologist, 22*(3), 316–335. doi: 10.1123/tsp.22.3.316

Hill, Y., den Hartigh, R. J. R., Meijer, R. R., de Jonge, P., & Van Yperen, N. W. (2018). Resilience in sports from a dynamical perspective. *Sport, Exercise and Performance Psychology, 7*(4), 333–341. doi: 10.1037/spy0000118

Hill, D. M., Matthews, N., & Senior, R. (2016). The psychological characteristics of performance under pressure in professional rugby union referees. *The Sport Psychologist, 30*(4), 376–387. doi: 10.1123/tsp.2015-0109

Jackson, J. W. (2002). Intergroup attitudes as a function of different dimensions of group identification and perceived intergroup conflict. *Self and Identity, 1*(1), 11–33. doi: 10.1080/152988602317232777

Kamans, E., Otten, S., & Gordijn, E. H. (2010). Power and threat in intergroup conflict: How emotional and behavioral responses depend on amount and content of threat. *Group Processes & Intergroup Relations, 14*(3), 293–310. doi: 10.1177/1368430210372525

Kellett, P., & Warner, S. (2011). Creating communities that lead to retention: The social worlds and communities of umpires. *European Sport Management Quarterly, 11*(5), 471–494. doi: 10.1080/16184742.2011.624109

Mäs, M., & Dijkstra, J. (2014). Do intergroup conflicts necessarily result from outgroup hate? *PLoS One, 9*(6), 1–19. doi: 1371/journal.pone.0097848

Mascarenhas, D., Collins, D., & Mortimer, R. L. (2005). A naturalistic approach to training accurate and coherent decision making in rugby union referees. *Sport Psychologist, 19*(2), 131–147. doi: 10.1123/tsp.19.2.131

Mascarenhas, D., O'Hare, D., & Plessner, H. (2006). The psychological and performance demands of association football refereeing. *International Journal of Sport Psychology, 37*(2/3), 99–120.

McDonald, M. M., Navarrete, D. C., & Van Vugt, M. (2012). Evolution and the psychology of intergroup conflict: The male warrior hypothesis. *Philosophical Transactions of the Royal Society B, 367*(1589), 670–679. doi: 10.1098/rstb.2011.0301

Nevill, A., Webb, T., & Watts, A. (2013). Improved training of football referees and the decline in home advantage post-WW2. *Psychology of Sport and Exercise, 14*(2), 220–227. doi: 10.1016/j.psychsport.2012.11.001

Pizzera, A., & Raab, M. (2012). Perceptual judgments of sports officials are influenced by their motor and visual experience. *Journal of Applied Sport Psychology, 24*(1), 59–72. doi: 10.1080/10413200.2011.608412

Ridinger, L. L. (2015). Contributors and constraints to involvement with youth sports officiating. *Journal of Amateur Sport, 1*(2), 103–127. doi: 10.17161/jas.v1i2.4946

Ridinger, L. L., Kim, K. R., Warner, S., & Tingle, J. K. (2017a). Development of the referee retention scale. *Journal of Sport Management, 31*(5), 514–527. doi: 10.1123/jsm.2017-0065

Ridinger, L. L., Warner, S., Tingle, J. K., & Kim, K. R. (2017b). Why referees stay in the game. *Global Sport Business Journal, 5*(3), 22–37.

Sarkar, M., & Fletcher, D. (2014). Psychological resilience in sport performers: A review of stressors and protective factors. *Journal of Sports Sciences, 32*(15), 1419–1434. doi: 10.1080/02640414.2014.901551

Slack, L. A., Maynard, I. W., Butt, J., & Olusoga, P. (2013). Factors underpinning elite sport officiating: Perceptions of English Premier League referees. *Journal of Applied Sport Psychology, 25*(3), 298–315. doi: 10.1080/10413200.2012.726935

Warner, S., Tingle, J. K., & Kellett, P. (2013). Officiating attrition: The experience of former referees via a sport development lens. *Journal of Sport Management, 27*(4), 316–328. doi: 10.1123/jsm.27.4.316

Webb, T. (2014). The emergence of training and assessment for referees in association football. *The International Journal of the History of Sport, 31*(9), 1081–1097. doi: 10.1080/09523367.2014.905545

Webb, T. (2016). "Knight of the whistle": W. P. Harper and the impact of the media on an association football referee. *The International Journal of the History of Sport, 33*(3), 306–324. doi: 10.1080/09523367.2016.1151004

Webb, T. (2017). *Elite soccer referees: Officiating in the Premier League, La Liga and Serie A.* London: Routledge.

Webb, T., Cleland, J. & O'Gorman, J. (2017). The distribution of power through a media campaign: The Respect programme, referees and violence in association football. *The Journal of Global Sport Management, 2*(3), 162-181

Webb, T. (2018). Managing match officials: The influence of business and the impact of finance in an era of Premier League dominance. In S. Chadwick, D. Parnell, P. Widdop, & C. Anagnostopoulos (Eds.), *Routledge handbook of football business and management* (pp. 366–375). London: Routledge.

Webb, T., Dicks, M., Thelwell, R., & Nevill, A. (2018). The impact of referee training: Reflections on the reduction of home advantage in association football. *Soccer & Society, 19*(7), 1024–1037. doi: 10.1080/14660970.2016.1267626

Webb, T., Rayner, M. & Thelwell, R. (2019). An examination of match official's perceptions of support and abuse in rugby union and cricket in England. *Managing Sport and Leisure, 24*(1-3), 155-172

Webb, T., Dicks, M., Thelwell, R., van der Kamp, J., & Rix-Lievre, G. (2020). An analysis of soccer referee experiences in France and the Netherlands: Abuse, conflict and level of support. *Sport Management Review, 23*(1), 52–65. doi: 10.1016/j.smr.2019.03.003

Webb, T., & Hill, D. M. (2020). The psychology of soccer referees. In J. Dixon, J. B. Barker, R. C. Thelwell, & I. Mitchell (Eds.), *The psychology of soccer.* London: Routledge.

Webb, T., Rayner, M., & Thelwell, R. (2019). An examination of match official's perceptions of support and abuse in rugby union and cricket in England. *Managing Sport and Leisure, 24*(1–3), 155–172. doi: 10.1080/23750472.2019.1605841

Weisel, O., & Böhm, R. (2015). "Ingroup love" and "outgroup hate" in intergroup conflict between natural groups. *Journal of Experimental Psychology, 60*, 110–120. doi: 10.1016/j.jesp.2015.04.00

Windle, G., Bennett, K. M., & Noyes, J. (2011). A methodological review of resilience measurement scales. *Health & Quality of Life Outcomes, 9*, 8–25. doi: 10.1186/1477-7525-9-8

5 The importance of policy and the need for mental health interventions and support

Introduction

The previous chapters in this book have considered a number of interconnected areas related to the environment and operational factors concerning match official abuse in English football, cricket, rugby union and rugby league. For example, the abuse itself has been a common narrative threaded throughout the previous chapters (in addition to a specific emphasis in Chapter 2), which have included a focus around organisational culture and discontinuation (Chapter 3), positive environments, resilience and managing conflict (Chapter 4), as well as good governance and the importance of effective support networks for match officials. Clearly all of these issues have the potential to impact upon match officials. It is reasonable to assume that these matters are not just confined to the sports we examine and potentially operate across numerous countries. What we do not understand is the impact of these negative situations on individual match officials.

What is known, however, is workplace stress, a lack of organisational support and abuse from others in the working environment are contributory factors to the development of poor mental health (Attridge, 2019). For example, studies focusing upon the nature of work and mental health have noted that a lack of social support and isolation at work can contribute to poor mental health of workers. Some workers also face trauma in the workplace from bullying, mobbing or having abusive colleagues. In addition, when employees perceive that the rewards are not commensurate with the effort they invest in their role, the risk of poor mental health increases (Wiencke, Cacace, & Fischer, 2016). Given the match officials in our surveys have conveyed exposure to and experience of such factors, a logical conclusion is their officiating roles potentially subject them to conditions that may negatively impact upon their mental health (Gouttebarge, Johnson, Rochcongar, Rosier, & Kerkhoffs, 2017).

Therefore, this chapter considers how policy can positively and negatively impact upon groups of match officials across sports in England particularly.

Suggested examples of policy interventions are provided and crucially, match officials' experiences, views and interpretations of their potential efficacy. It also addresses the importance of good mental health, identifying solutions to some of the issues raised and examining how these solutions might better support match officials, given the abuse to which they are exposed. Initially the effect of abuse and poor mental health is considered, building on the extant research in the field of mental health in sport.

Mental health and sport

We often hear discussions surrounding mental health in sport, although very often they do not provide definitions or outcomes for performers. This lack of a unified definition means that those involved in sport (players, coaches and match officials predominantly) have a level of disjointed support at best and, at worst, no support at all. In the context of this book, we contend that sports match officials are arguably individuals who require greater mental health knowledge and support than other groups in sport. They often operate in isolation at lower levels of sport, coupled with exposure to abusive situations or environments which requires specific support in order to operate effectively. In order to contextualise mental health support for match officials, we must initially understand what constitutes good mental health and also the current literature and initiatives related to this topic in sport.

Mental illnesses, as opposed to mental health, can be described as diagnosed conditions that comprise of changes in emotions, thinking and behaving, and often lead to distress and issues around functioning in social situations (American Psychiatric Association, 2013). The Mental Health Foundation (n.d.), based in the United Kingdom (UK), states that:

> good mental health is fundamental to thriving in life. It is the essence of who we are and how we experience the world. Yet, compared to physical health, so little is commonly known about mental ill health and how to prevent it.

Mind, a UK based mental health charity, identifies that mental health problems in England and Wales are increasing and predicted that by 2020 depression will be the leading cause of health problems in Europe, with the current cost of poor mental health to UK society in excess of £110 billion (Mind, 2012).

In sport, much of the literature and the wider focus has been on athletes and the physical demands of sport, rather than the athletes' mental health (Rice et al., 2016). However, Gouttebarge et al. (2019) considered the prevalence of mental health symptoms and disorders in current and former elite athletes, and there is a recent burgeoning literature around athletes' mental health (see for example Bauman, 2016; Gulliver, Griffiths, Mackinnon, Batterham, & Stanimirovic, 2015; Schinke, Stambulova, & Zella Moore, 2018). Conversely, comparatively little mental health research has concentrated on sports match officials, with some notable exceptions (Gorczynski & Webb, 2020; Gouttebarge et al., 2017; Kilic, Johnson, Kerkhoffs, Rosier, & Gouttebarge, 2018). In order to perform effectively, match officials need to be in optimum condition in terms of their personal, physical and psychological health. However, as discussed in Chapters 2 and 3, a significant number of match officials have been exposed to stressful situations which have included abusive threats towards their physical and psychological wellbeing over a prolonged period of time (Voight, 2009; Webb, Cleland, & O'Gorman, 2017; Webb, Rayner, & Thelwell, 2018).

The current situation creates a dichotomy for match officials, between their love for the game and wanting to officiate, and the challenging circumstances, environments and situations in which they can often find themselves. The operational environment in which football referees perform, for example, is constantly changing, both at the elite level of sport or the grassroots game where the vast majority of referees operate (Webb, 2017). There is also a lack of understanding regarding the match official workforces across sports and across countries, despite recent advancements in academic literature (Cleland, O'Gorman, & Bond, 2015; Cleland, O'Gorman, & Webb, 2018; Ridinger, Kim, Warner, & Tingle, 2017a; Ridinger, Warner, Tingle, & Kim, 2017b; Webb, 2018; Webb et al., 2017; Webb & Thelwell, 2015) as well as in the work that is being undertaken directly by the governing bodies of sport.

Recent initiatives have been launched by English governing bodies. For example, the FA alongside Heads Together, a mental health charity with The Royal Foundation of The Duke and Duchess of Cambridge and The Duke and Duchess of Sussex, have launched the "Heads Up" initiative, designed to prioritise mental fitness as much as physical fitness, facilitating the "biggest conversation ever around mental health" (The FA, n.d.). However, the "Heads Up" initiative, when launched, was focused around players, with the handbook produced as part of the campaign particularly aimed at providing information for coaches and managers. Although referees are mentioned briefly on page 9 of the handbook (The FA, 2019), there is no other direction for coaches and managers to assist in dealing with the mental health of referees. Indeed, it is arguable whether coaches and managers are the most appropriate individuals to identify poor mental health in referees or match officials at all, particularly given the historically fractious relationship that exists (Cleland et al., 2018; Ridinger, 2015; Webb, Dicks, Thelwell, van der Kamp, & Rix-Lievre, 2020; Webb, Rayner, & Thelwell, 2019).

However, in 2020 the mental health guidance notes for referees was released, as part of the wider "Heads Up" campaign by the FA. It was the intention of the mental health guidance notes to provide referees, and those involved with refereeing, a handbook to enable them to spot the signs of any mental health concerns, feel confident to report those concerns and subsequently be able to signpost people to the appropriate places for help (The FA, 2020). The document also explains what mental health is, why it is being raised and discussed, examples of signs to be able to identify reduced mental health, organisations that can help when mental health concerns, as well as examples from referees and those involved in refereeing (The FA, 2020).

The Rugby Football League and the charity State of Mind, meanwhile, launched the State of Mind programme in 2011, aimed at improving the mental health, wellbeing and working life of rugby league players and communities (The RFL, n.d.). Following the initial launch of the project in the UK Super League, State of Mind is now an international charity and works across sports including rugby union, with specific pages of the RFU website dedicated to mental health literacy and support (The RFU, n.d.). Additionally, a further initiative, "Offload", has been launched by the Rugby League Cares charity, designed to challenge how sport addresses issues such as depression and anxiety (What is Offload?, n.d.). The "Offload" initiative addresses and supports men's mental fitness and wellbeing in partnership with State of Mind and the foundations at Salford Red Devils, Warrington Wolves and Widnes Vikings.

However, despite the aims and objectives of the State of Mind project and the "Offload" initiative, the primary intention, certainly initially, was to engage with players rather than match officials. This situation is starting to change with State of Mind recently invited to speak at referees' societies (State of Mind, 2019), with a potential catalyst being the former Super League referee Ian Smith admitting that he often felt isolated and lonely during matches, principally due to the pressure that rugby league referees are under from other stakeholders, such as owners, players, coaches and supporters (Woods, 2017).

"Sport has a long way to go"

In terms of mental health provision and support in sport, the argument persists that although significant developments and advancements have been made, there is still "a long way to go" (Lovett, 2019). Moreover, the players or athletes themselves have helped the developments that have been made through the communication of their experiences, with the Professional Cricketers' Association, Rugby Players' Association and Professional Footballers' Association in the UK all overseeing an increase in their members accessing support (Lovett, 2019).

In 2018 the UK government, through the Department for Digital, Culture, Media and Sport (DCMS), launched the Mental Health and Elite Sport Action Plan, intended to improve support for elite athletes. Additionally, the DCMS publication *Sporting Future – A New Strategy for an Active Nation*, focused on the prominence of wellbeing and understanding the sacrifices that elite athletes make to achieve success (DCMS, 2015). This document was followed by the launch in 2018 of the "*Mental Health Charter for Sport and Recreation*", a written commitment from sporting organisations, such as national governing bodies of sport (NGBs), through the Sport and Recreation Alliance, the representative body for national sports organisations in the UK. The charter outlines how sport and recreation groups should adopt good mental health practice guaranteeing that activities are inclusive.

Other sporting organisations have also begun to focus more explicitly on the impact of both good and poor mental health on athletes. UK Sport and the English Institute of Sport (EIS) announced a programme of mental health education, aimed at supporting athletes and promoting positive mental health across the high-performance system in the UK (UK Sport, 2019). In particular the programme is designed to reach all 1,200 world class athletes leading up to the next Olympics to be held in Tokyo, with the EIS recruiting a Head of Mental Health in 2018 to support and facilitate the aims and objectives of the programme (EIS, 2018). Specifically, the focus is on:

- Facilitating a performance environment that considers the whole person, aiming to develop athletes as people and not just performers.
- Constructing a working environment promoting informed choice and autonomy.
- Developing and maintaining connections with people inside and outside of the elite sport environment.
- Fostering a culture that prioritises mental recovery in the physical training environment.

(UK Sport, 2019)

Nevertheless, despite all of these recent advancements in sport, match officials are side-lined and often not included. Thus, there is a lack of focus on the needs and requirements of match officials across sports and therefore this chapter now focuses on the associated pressures which might contribute to mental health concerns, and the wider societal, environmental and personal factors influencing match official welfare. We also consider the future outcomes derived from our understanding following the research conducted with match officials evidenced in this book, and also other previous research (Webb, 2017; Webb et al., 2017, 2019, 2020; Webb & Gorczynski, in press).

Match officials and mental health concerns

Figure 5.1, the Conceptual model of the factors influencing match official welfare and future outcomes, identifies societal, environmental and personal factors which impact upon match official welfare. A number of factors are relevant at both grassroots and elite level sport, such as the personal factors aspect of the conceptual model. The particular standard of sport and therefore the level that match officials officiate can also be affected by environmental factors. As match officials progress through their respective officiating levels, dependent on their chosen sport, societal factors can also impact upon match officials. Different societal factors such as the implications of any decisions made, and the resultant media interest and television coverage as a result of these decisions, all have an influence on elite match official welfare. This is due, principally, to the extent of any media coverage and the associated exposure at national and international levels, which is more applicable to elite level match officials than those operating at the grassroots level, although there can still be an impact irrespective of level (Webb, 2017).

At the lower levels of sport, societal factors such as the behaviour of players, coaches and spectators can affect match officials. For example, any negative behaviour can lead to significant verbal and physical abuse directed towards the match official, and an associated impact on retention levels within the sport in question (Webb et al., 2017). At the higher levels of sport there is less chance of this verbal abuse increasing to physical abuse

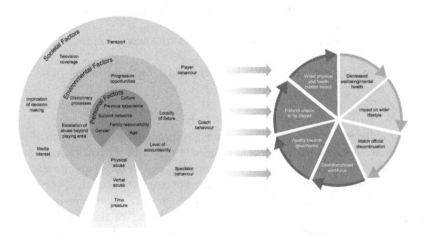

Figure 5.1 Conceptual model of the factors influencing match official welfare and future outcomes

and continuing after the match has finished, due to the security and police presence in place in professional sport (Cleland et al., 2018; Webb, 2017). In elite sport, the coverage of any high-profile incidents can also influence the behaviour of players, coaches and spectators at lower levels of sport through the imitation of abusive or aggressive behaviour (Webb, 2017). The conceptual model outlined in Figure 5.1 recognises that both verbal and physical abuse, and the associated pressure, influence the personal factors related to match officials and can negatively impact upon their mental health, leading to indifference towards governance and a marginalised workforce, which can lead to further match official discontinuation (Ridinger et al., 2017b).

Across our research, match officials identified that any improvements which can be viewed as beneficial to their mental health and wellbeing must begin with enhancements to the environment in which they operate. Until the environment and the culture around sport shifts and accepts match officials are part of the game, and not an 'outgroup' that are 'fair game' to act abusively or aggressively towards, it is difficult to envisage how this might change. For example, match officials argued that there should be a concerted and informed approach to a lack of respect, particularly in football. One football referee (male, 6–10 years' experience, 35–44 age group), a voice of many referees, believed that this respect must be demonstrated at the elite level of the game for there to be any influence in grassroots sport:

> There must be strong messages from the FA and the Referees Association to ensure that where there is a lack of respect it is dealt with firmly. If this is demonstrated at senior level it will be seen by those at grass roots level and the culture will change for the better.

Another football referee (male, 11–15 years' experience, 45–54 age group) suggested that those in positions of governance should go further and be supported by both the FA and FIFA in order to effect real and meaningful change: "Only when the top Premier League and international referees get tougher on bad behaviour and more importantly get backed up by the FA and FIFA will anything change". Interestingly, other examples from the data identified that football referees also believed that the problem is players' perceptions of referees and having a right to treat referees in an abusive way. By way of illustration was this response by a male (11–15 years' experience, 55–64 age group) referee:

> Those few people who, whatever their connection with football see a referee as someone who they have a "right" to abuse in whatever form they choose. As a referee all we can do is use the laws of the game to

deal with the lack of respect by players and coaches when it becomes too much. If they cannot respect the job we do for them to ensure a fair match then we have no choice – and people wonder why the game struggles to attract new refs! Thankfully I do not let it get to me, BUT it would improve my 90 minutes if I did not have to deal/endure their lack of self-control. This is a very deep-seated problem.

For this referee, he believed he could cope with the abuse to which he was subjected, although other match officials or referees might not consider themselves as mentally strong. If compared to other workplace settings in which workers find themselves in similarly abusive workplace situations (Wiencke et al., 2016), this abuse could have a far more deleterious impact upon their mental health and wellbeing. Another football referee (male, 11–15 years' experience, 35–44 age group) argued that there should be greater attention paid to the support around referees, as well as the blame that is attached to referee decisions in football at higher levels of the game. Moreover, the argument was made that the role of the club welfare officers should be extended and that this would help to support referees:

> We need much greater hands on support from the FA, such as mentors or critical friends who attend matches where there's been issues. Having less high-profile figures in football blaming the referees on tv, this just creates the norm that it's ok to blame the ref and it filters down to lower levels. We should also be extending the role and number of the welfare officer in clubs who have a responsibility to randomly observe conduct at games, provide feedback to teams on their behaviour, report to the FA and to support the referees. Many of these referees are children themselves, who are quite frankly experiencing abuse at times, which could also develop into more personal issues for these referees.

The suggested increased hands-on support requested by match officials of the English FA can manifest itself in a number of ways. The preceding referee, representing a number of referees from our data, believed that mentors were an important part of the support network for referees, helping to support their mental health and wellbeing. Football referees believed that despite some marginal gains in the way that referees are treated, the abuse and the consequences of that abuse for individual referees remained a primary concern. Education was believed to be a method for increasing understanding around the role that referees play in football, although it was also intimated that the culture of abuse and attitude towards referees was a wider societal concern. One referee (male, 21+ years' experience, 55–64 age group) argued that slogans and campaigns are not going to change the issues that referees face and that education is the only way to effect real change: "Slogans are useless. Educate the idiots who are supposed to, but are not, setting the right example. And I stress this is not just a problem with attitudes to referees, it is bigger than that".

There are opportunities to learn from other sports in this scenario. For example, match officials believed that there is less tolerance of abuse in rugby union compared to football, and there is certainly an historical argument to support this notion (Webb, 2016; Webb et al., 2019). One referee (female, 6–10 years' experience, 25–34 age group) argued that "the FA should adopt the rugby union stance on respect . . . address the bullying of referees by players and officials . . . a referee is not and should not be trying to win a 'popularity contest', they should be allowed to do their job". However, although we can see in earlier chapters (see Chapters 2 and 3) that there is less of a concern regarding abuse and the treatment of referees in rugby union, we also know that there are still issues related to abuse which require attention (Rayner, Webb, & Webb, 2016; Webb et al., 2019).

In rugby league, alongside the partnership with State of Mind, there has arguably been the most concerted focus on the wellbeing of athletes in sport in England. This has started to extend to referees more recently, although this is still not at the level that referees would expect and that would assist the recruitment and retention of referees, as illustrated by this referee (rugby league referee, male, 6–10 years' experience, 18–24 age group):

> I feel that rugby league in general is taking big steps regarding player welfare and depression. However, the referee side needs looking into, especially with the amount of abuse and criticism referees come under from spectators and coaches. This has improved a little . . . but improvement is still needed.

Despite the advancements made in the wider game of rugby league, some referees believed that they are not receiving the same amount or level of support. Arguably match officials are the individuals in sport who require increased support and consideration of their wider wellbeing and mental health, particularly given the abuse to which they are subjected. Across sports, it is apparent that structures and policies around player welfare are developing and evolving, and yet for match officials this support is still in its infancy. At the higher levels of elite sport pressure exists through the media's public influence of their decisions. The decisions of a match official can alter the course of a match and, at times, be the difference between winning and losing for teams, players and coaches. At the lower levels pressure also exists. Match officials can feel under pressure as a result of the environment in which they are operating. They might be the only match official, officiating a match between two teams, with coaches, substitutes and supporters, and the match official is therefore an isolated arbiter of the laws of the game, open to potential issues if decisions are not well received by those playing, coaching or spectating. In football, for example, it has been recognised that providing support is essential for referees at lower levels of the game, particularly young or new referees. This female referee (3–5 years' experience, 18–24 age group) exemplified the issues around young referees: "In grassroots football there are young female referees, there are young male referees, that may find it difficult to talk or even have that support . . . we definitely need to be there for them . . . they need that support".

Nevertheless, in football, it is recognised that the support and structures around referees are improving, albeit at a slower rate than those involved in officiating would like to see:

> In football I would say it's slowly getting better. I think that's purely from ex professional referees and players stepping out and saying, 'I've had to deal with mental health' and you know all the documentaries on TV and people being open about things, that's kind of helped . . . referees in comparison to footballers we need it, we need mental health support a lot more.
> (Football referee, female, 3–5 years' experience, 18–24 age group)

Much of the outlook articulated by the referee in the quotation, and from many other referees we could have used here, can also be applied to other sports. The provision of mental health services and support is not currently as prevalent for match officials. Earlier in this chapter we examined the mental health and wellbeing provision in football, rugby union and rugby league and it is evident that there is far greater attention paid to other stakeholder groups, rather than referees. The question then becomes how can we better support match officials, and what can be done to assist any improvements in both their operational environment and their individual and group wellbeing/mental health?

Supporting match officials – mentoring

Match officials and their wellbeing and mental health can be supported in a number of ways. We know that if a match official is subjected to verbal and physical abuse, there may be a consequence as a result of this abuse, dependent on the mental toughness and resilience of the match official in question. However, the provision of mentors can be a way of supporting match officials when this support is required. For example, some rugby union referees, like the one who follows, identified the importance of mentors, and how mentors and mentees can benefit from this relationship:

I strongly believe that having a mentor is beneficial both for the mentor and for the referee mentored; follow to games, do video review together, share and exchange experiences and learn from best practise as well as in learning giving feedback and coaching.

(Rugby union referee, female, 3–5 years'
experience, 25–34 age group)

Issues arise when support is not forthcoming and therefore, referee welfare can be overlooked. Rugby union referees identified that there simply are not enough individuals who are willing to act as mentors and support referees. One referee (male, 21+ years' experience, 55–64 age group) outlined the lack of individuals who are in support roles, citing time pressure as one reason why it is difficult to attract people: "Apart from monthly meetings, there are not enough people to support the frontline referees. If I don't ask for help it wouldn't be forthcoming at all. It is all down to time pressures". Despite the identification of mentoring as a positive process which can help match officials, in rugby union it is also recognised that the provision of mentors can be problematic to organise and to facilitate effectively, particularly when considering the number of mentees that are required. For example, if we take rugby union as an illustration, every year the RFU recruit approximately 2,000 new referees in England (Wilson, 2016). If a mentor was appointed to every new referee, even if a mentor had five mentees each, this would still require 400 mentors for these new referees. This would be a fluid and evolving mentee workforce given the turnover of referees, and therefore it demonstrates a significant undertaking season upon season for the RFU and the regional referee societies throughout the country.

In cricket, some umpires believed that they were often well supported, although there was also room for this support to be increased, both from those who train and develop match officials and the match officials themselves. This was illustrated in the following extract:

Umpires are generally well supported in their training but need greater practical support once they have begun to be active and as they progress through their careers. Some umpires also need to take greater responsibility for updating their skills and knowledge once they have qualified.

(Cricket umpire, male, 16–20 years'
experience, 55–64 age group)

Cricket umpires have tried to further increase this support by forming informal groups, as a way of dealing with some of the pressures and associated wellbeing issues which they subsequently face. This also means that any support and welfare related activity can be localised such as this response by a male cricket umpire (6–10 years' experience, 55–64 age group): "I am a member of a 'more' local group of umpires which meet informally on a monthly basis that I believe enables umpires to support each other more effectively, than just a regional or national group can do". Conversely, the notion of individual responsibility is considered further by cricket umpires, who believed that they also need to stop living in the past and embrace the structural, governance-related changes and developments that have occurred recently in cricket, including too much focus on local associations:

> There are still individual umpires and some in authority who are living in the past and who have not properly embraced the ECB Association of Cricket Officials (ACO) as an organisation whilst choosing to immerse themselves in local associations whose objectives and values are out of date.
>
> (Cricket umpire, male, 11–15 years' experience, 55–64 age group)

The umpire argued that there are still umpires and individuals in positions of authority who have not embraced recent changes in the organisation and support network. In particular it was claimed that the ACO, responsible for the recruitment, training and development of cricket match officials, has not been fully accepted, as umpires still tend to gravitate towards local associations perceived to have outdated approaches.

In many sports mentoring has been utilised for match officials. However, one of the issues across sport are the number of mentors available, meaning that match officials will have varied experiences and an inconsistent support network on which they can rely. Furthermore, across different sports there is little direct consideration of mental health or wellbeing issues for match officials. This could be a sign that historically this topic is not particularly well covered, and the recent campaigns and initiatives identified towards the start of this chapter have confirmed that match officials have received very little thought or coverage in these programmes. Therefore, it is perhaps unsurprising that match officials are not openly discussing or mentioning mental health or wellbeing initiatives or training provision. In short, they simply do not currently exist at the time of writing.

The absence of appreciation and empathy for match officials

So far, this chapter has focused on the provision of mental health support for sports match officials and the need for this provision to increase and evolve and identified mentoring as an essential support mechanism for those match officials who have experienced verbal and/or physical abuse. However, we also argue here for a step change, for a cultural shift in the way that match officials in sport are treated, governed and managed. We highlight the need for change in the way that match officials are viewed by other groups or stakeholders within their sport, namely players, coaches and spectators. We request that personal and group actions are considered, that the individual match official's mental health and wellbeing is recognised and promoted and that if something happens to those individuals, such as if they are verbally or physically assaulted, that they are provided with the correct training and support to deal with and move on from the issue. We also ask that punishments are commensurate for the action which has transpired. Namely, if an individual acts in a negative or threatening way towards a match official, they are dealt with by the appropriate disciplinary procedures administered by the respective national governing bodies.

To achieve any of this, there is a fundamental requirement that change is instigated. We know how and why match officials discontinue, but the next step is to support them more effectively, provide more coherent structures for this support and provide education, in terms of mental health literacy, for both match officials and also players, coaches and spectators. This proposed education for players, coaches and spectators would focus upon the impact of their actions on the match officials in question, and how changes in attitude and behaviour could improve relationships between match officials and players, coaches and spectators, as well as positively impacting upon match official recruitment and retention. This raises another question, such as whether we expect too much from match officials. The drive for perfection in decision making is driven by the almost forensic analysis which now exists in elite sport. The relationship between sport and the media, the development of technology and the consanguinity of this technology within live sport programmes as well as highlights programmes, has led to unprecedented coverage of referee performances and their decision making process (Webb, 2016, 2018).

This increased coverage and relationship with the media has brought unintended consequences for match officials at varying levels of sport. At the elite level, we know the increased pressure that this relationship brings; however at lower levels this can also have an impact on the behaviour of players, coaches and spectators. The drive for excellence in elite level sport has meant that individuals who play, coach or watch local sport expect the match official to be at the equivalent level as those that are seen on televised sport (Webb et al., 2017). Hence, there are unrealistic expectations on match officials at lower levels of sport, and there are also consequences of any televised negative behaviour towards match officials. This behaviour, once observed on television, can be replicated in local sport the following weekend, creating even more challenging environments and conditions for the respective match officials (Webb et al., 2019). Cricket umpires believed that a greater appreciation of their role would be advantageous. In particular, one umpire (male, 3–5 years' experience, 55–64 age group) identified that further engagement with players would help the situation: "A more concerted attempt at player training, making captains more aware of their responsibilities". For other cricket umpires, such as this one (male, 11–15 years' experience, 45–54 age group), this potential change would attempt to alter some of these dynamics:

> The introduction of an umpiring appreciation course for players (especially Captains) – simple examples of this need are the impatience shown by Captains at the toss whilst essential matters (such as local rules, the judging of wides, agreeing scheduled breaks, covering the pitch in inclement weather & age-group player identification) are discussed.

It appears that some of the issues between professional match officials, players and coaches and those operating at lower levels of each respective sport can be attributed to a disconnect. This leads to match officials observing and experiencing issues with players and attempting to manage their expectations. Match officials themselves acknowledge that there can be inconsistencies between the levels at which they operate, and that this may lead to some of the issues between match officials, players and coaches, in particular. Rugby referees identified that the consistency of training and support could be more standardised, believing that this would help match officials and their relationships with coaches and players. Representing a number of rugby union referees on this subject was the following extract:

> There needs to be consistency at every level from 12 to the Premiership. At the moment, I'm a level 5 referee. However, the protocols for a referee to follow are different to those of a national panel referee. As a result, I am uncertain of what assessors want from my performance.
> (Rugby union referee, male, 3–5 years' experience,
> 18–24 age group)

Despite the identification of consistency as a potential solution to the issues that exist between match officials, players, coaches and spectators, other rugby union referees believed that there must also be some consideration that no two match officials or referees are the same, and therefore, there will still be issues, even if a standardised protocol or approach was taken to any confrontational incidents:

> I don't think there is an easy answer. Individual referees have strengths and weaknesses, so each person deals with situations in their own way (rightly or wrongly). Each time there is an issue is it partly of the

referees own making by not dealing with problems, and players then get frustrated?

(Rugby union referee, male, 16–20 years'
experience, 45–54 age group)

Neither match officials, players, coaches nor spectators would be assisted by individual referees operating independently, or not following the procedures and protocols that have been set in place through the laws of the games and guidance from governing bodies. Indeed, match officials should evaluate whether their actions and performances could be improved in certain situations, and with a focus on the relationships between the relevant actors/ stakeholders. This evaluation and reflection could assist in an improvement in associated relationships. However, an accepted and uniform approach to situations, decision making and dealing with players, coaches and spectators would also improve these relationships. Moreover, one potential method of achieving this standardisation could be the provision of standard packs of training for referees, providing essential materials that are requiring match officials to operate uniformly, something which often does not occur routinely in sport (Webb, 2017). This rugby union referee (male, 16–20 years' experience, 45–54 age group) believed that the greater attendance of role models at training events would assist with recruitment and retention:

I can't believe that the RFU/England rugby do not provide standard 'packs' of training material that can be used by societies if they want to. They should also provide 1–2 'stars' (refs or players) per season to attend society training meetings as these attract people to the sessions and help with recruitment.

Conclusion

There are no easy solutions to the perception and treatment of match officials from players, coaches and spectators. However, it is clear that the current status quo is not sustainable. If the situation is allowed to continue and match officials are treated similarly over the next 10–15 years, a greater number of sporting fixtures every weekend in England and also more widely around the world, will take place without a qualified match official, or, a more likely scenario perhaps, these fixtures will not take place at all. A cultural change is required, and an improved understanding of the role that match officials provide to their sport is essential. There should be educational information around the role of match officials for all stakeholders, as well as the impact of any abuse or negative behaviour towards match officials, both individually and as a group. Only with a step change in this understanding and consequently an improved appreciation of match officials will instances of negative behaviour start to be reduced.

This chapter has concentrated upon the role of policy, and the wellbeing and mental health of English match officials involved in football, cricket, rugby union and rugby league. The focus on wellbeing and mental health in sport is improving, and there are a number of organisations and schemes in existence in different sports, designed to tackle mental health-related issues. However, it is also true to state that whilst these provisions for coaches and particularly players have improved, match officials are not receiving the same level of focus and support in this area. There are concerns for match officials, particularly given the abuse to which they are exposed, and the often-isolating outgroup environment that they operate within, as opposed to players, coaches and spectators who form the ingroup, as discussed in Chapter 4. All of this makes match officials a group of people in sport who require an improved standard of wellbeing and mental health support.

In order to better understand some of the challenges faced by match officials, and to identify variables which can influence their behaviour and intentions, we introduced the conceptual model of the factors influencing match official welfare and future outcomes (Figure 5.1). This model can be seen as a method of summarising and grouping the personal, environmental and societal factors that can influence match officials. This model is designed to change, evolve and refresh as the landscape in which match officials operate shifts and changes.

Across this chapter we have illustrated that sport has a long way to go before a progressive level of wellbeing and mental health support exists for match officials. There are associated challenges, such as a lack of appreciation and empathy for match officials across sports and a lack of formalised mentoring programmes. Mentoring has been suggested by the majority of match officials surveyed as an intervention that may benefit the support of officials' wellbeing. However, there are difficulties with the formation of successful mentoring programmes, not least the recruitment of relevant and correct mentors, and the training and placement of these mentors with appropriate mentees. The dynamic of this relationship is very important to any success that can be attributed to the respective programmes in football, cricket, rugby union and rugby league in England.

In light of the content covered in the present chapter and the investigation of the extant landscape in England, Chapter 6 focuses on the experiences of match officials outside England, where abuse and maltreatment of match officials also exists. It concentrates on the research, literature and media reports from countries across the world in order to better understand the extent of the problem. Research in this subject area outside the UK tends to emanate from the United States, Australia and New Zealand, and the subsequent chapter utilises research from these countries, alongside research conducted in France and the Netherlands to illustrate the trends across countries and sports.

References

American Psychiatric Association. (2013). *Diagnostic and statistical manual of mental disorders* (5th Ed.). Arlington, VA: American Psychiatric Publishing.

Attridge, M. (2019). A global perspective on promoting workplace mental health and the role of employee assistance programs. *American Journal of Health Promotion, 33*(4), 622–629. doi: 10.1177/0890117119838101c

Bauman, N. J. (2016). The stigma of mental health in athletes: Are mental toughness and mental health seen as contradictory in elite sport? *British Journal of Sports Medicine, 50*, 135–136. doi: 10.1136/bjsports-2015-095570

Cleland, J., O'Gorman, J., & Bond, M. (2015). The English football association's respect campaign: The referees' view. *International Journal of Sport, Policy and Politics, 7*(4), 551–563. doi: 10.1080/19406940.2015.1088050

Cleland, J., O'Gorman, J., & Webb, T. (2018). Respect? An investigation into the experience of referees in association football. *The International Review for the Sociology of Sport, 53*(8), 960–974. doi: 10.1177/1012690216687979

DCMS. (2015). *Sporting future: A new strategy for an active nation.* London: Sport England.

EIS. (2018). *EIS recruiting head of mental health.* Retrieved from www.eis2win.co.uk/article/eis-recruiting-head-of-mental-health/

The FA. (n.d.). *Heads up: About heads up.* Retrieved from www.thefa.com/about-football-association/heads-up

The FA. (2019). *Mental health, spotting the signs, supporting, signposting: For coaches and managers in adult football clubs.* Retrieved from www.thefa.com/about-football-association/heads-up

The FA. (2020). *The FA mental health guidance notes for referees.* Retrieved from www.thefa.com/news/2020/feb/05/referee-mental-health-guidance-notes-lucy-briggs-account-060220

Gorczynski, P. & Webb, T. (2020). Call to action: The need for a mental health research agenda for sports match officials. Managing Sport and Leisure. doi: 10.1080/237540472.2020.1792803

Gouttebarge, V., Johnson, U., Rochcongar, P., Rosier, P., & Kerkhoffs, G. (2017). Symptoms of common mental disorders among professional football referees: A one-season prospective study across Europe. *The Physician and Sports Medicine, 45*(1), 11–16. doi: 10.1080/00913847.2017.1248796

Gouttebarge, V., Castaldelli-Maia, J. M., Gorczynski, P., Hainline, B., Hitchcock, M. E., Kerkhoffs, G. M., Rice, S. M., Claudia, L., & Reardon, C. L. (2019). Occurrence of mental health symptoms and disorders in current and former elite athletes: A systematic review and meta-analysis. British Journal of Sports Medicine, 53(11), 700–706.

Gulliver, A., Griffiths, K. M., Mackinnon, A., Batterham, P. J., & Stanimirovic, R. (2015). The mental health of Australian elite athletes. *Journal of Science and Medicine in Sport, 18*(3), 255–261. doi: 10.1016/j.jsams.2014.04.006

Kilic, O., Johnson, U., Kerkhoffs, G. M. M. J., Rosier, P., & Gouttebarge, V. (2018). Exposure to physical and psychosocial stressors in relation to symptoms of common mental disorders among European professional football referees: A prospective cohort study. *British Medical Journal, 4*(1). doi: 10.1136/bmjsem-2017-000306

Lovett, S. (2019). *Sport has made much progress in the field of mental health-but there's still a long way to go*. Retrieved from www.independent.co.uk/sport/the-sporting-mind-series-mental-health-sport-fa-pfa-pca-rpa-a8945361.html

Mental Health Foundation. (n.d.). *Good mental health for all*. Retrieved from www.mentalhealth.org.uk/sites/default/files/who-we-are-2016.pdf

Mind. (2012). *Unstoppable together: The mind strategy 2012–2016, executive summary*. Retrieved from www.mind.org.uk/media/195849/External_2012-16_strategy_summary.pdf

Rayner, M., Webb, T., & Webb, H. (2016). The occurrence of referee abuse in rugby union: Evidence and measures through an online survey. *International Journal of Sport Management, Recreation and Tourism, 21*(d), 66–81. doi: doi.org/10.5199/ijsmart-1791-874X-21d

The RFL. (n.d.). *State of mind*. Retrieved from www.rugby-league.com/the_rfl/equality__diversity/state_of_mind

The RFU. (n.d.). *Mental health and wellbeing*. Retrieved from www.englandrugby.com/participation/playing/player-welfare-rugby-safe/mental-health-and-wellbeing

Rice, S. M., Purcell, R., De Silva, S., Mawren, D., McGorry, P. D., & Parker, A. G. (2016). The mental health of elite athletes: A narrative systematic review. *Sports Medicine, 46*(9), 1333–1353. doi: 10.1007/s40279-016-0492-2

Ridinger, L. L. (2015). Contributors and constraints to involvement with youth sports officiating. *Journal of Amateur Sport, 1*(2), 103–127. doi: 10.17161/jas.v1i2.4946

Ridinger, L. L., Kim, K. R., Warner, S., & Tingle, J. K. (2017a). Development of the referee retention scale. *Journal of Sport Management, 31*(5), 514–527. doi: 10.1123/jsm.2017-0065

Ridinger, L. L., Warner, S., Tingle, J. K., & Kim, K. R. (2017b). Why referees stay in the game. *Global Sport Business Journal, 5*(3), 22–37.

Schinke, R. J., Stambulova, N. B., & Zella Moore, G. (2018). International society of sport psychology position stand: Athletes' mental health, performance, and development. *International Journal of Sport and Exercise Psychology, 16*(6), 622–639. doi: 10.1080/1612197X.2017.1295557

State of Mind. (2019). *State of mind with hull referees society*. Retrieved from https://stateofmindsport.org/post/state-of-mind-with-hull-referees-society/

UK Sport. (2019). *Mental health education programme aims to support every athlete and promote positive mental health*. Retrieved from www.uksport.gov.uk/news/2019/05/13/mental-health-education-programme-aims-to-support-every-athlete

Voight, M. (2009). Sources of stress and coping strategies of US soccer officials. *Stress & Health, 25*(1), 91–101. doi: 10.1002/smi.1231

Webb, T. (2016). "Knight of the whistle": W. P. Harper and the impact of the media on an association football referee. *The International Journal of the History of Sport, 33*(3), 306–324. doi: 10.1080/09523367.2016.1151004

Webb, T. (2017). *Elite soccer referees: Officiating in the Premier League, La Liga and Serie A*. London: Routledge.

Webb, T. (2018). Referees and the media: A difficult relationship but an unavoidable necessity.*Soccer&Society,19*(2),205–221.doi:10.1080/14660970.2015.1133414.

Webb, T., Cleland, J., & O'Gorman, J. (2017). The distribution of power through a media campaign: The respect programme, referees and violence in association football. *The Journal of Global Sport Management, 2*(3), 162–181. doi: 10.1080/24704067.2017.1350591

Webb, T., Dicks, M., Thelwell, R., van der Kamp, J., & Rix-Lievre, G. (2020). An analysis of soccer referee experiences in France and the Netherlands: Abuse, conflict, and support. *Sport Management Review, 23*(1), 52–65. doi: 10.1016/j.smr.2019.03.003

Webb, T., & Gorczynski, P. (in press). Factors influencing the mental health of sports match officials: The potential impact of abuse and a destabilised support system from a global context. In M. Lang (Ed.), *The international handbook of athlete welfare*. London: Routledge.

Webb, T., Rayner, M., & Thelwell, R. (2018). An explorative case study of referee abuse in English Rugby League. *Journal of Applied Sport Management, 10*(2), doi: 10.18666/JASM-2017-V10-12-8834

Webb, T., Rayner, M., & Thelwell, R. (2019). An examination of match official's perceptions of support and abuse in rugby union and cricket in England. *Managing Sport and Leisure, 24*(1–3), 155–172. doi: 10.1080/23750472.2019.1605841

Webb, T., & Thelwell, R. (2015). "He's taken a dive": Cultural comparisons of elite referee responses to reduced player behaviour in association football. *Sport, Business and Management: An International Journal, 5*(3), 242–258. doi: 10.1108/SBM-04-2014-0019

What is Offload?. (n.d.). Retrieved from www.rugbyleaguecares.org/what-we-do/health-and-wellbeing/offload/what-is-offload/

Wiencke, M., Cacace, M., & Fischer, S. (Eds.). (2016). *Healthy at work: Interdisciplinary perspectives*. Switzerland: Springer.

Wilson, J. (2016). *Exclusive: Rugby's values at threat as verbal and physical abuse of referees is on the rise*. Retrieved from www.telegraph.co.uk/rugby-union/2016/03/22/rugbys-values-at-threat-as-instances-of-verbal-and-physical-abus/

Woods, D. (2017). *Ian Smith: Former referee says he often felt "lonely and isolated" during matches*. Retrieved from www.bbc.co.uk/sport/rugby-league/40246318

6 The experience of match officials outside England

Introduction

Previous chapters in this book have predominantly considered the experiences of match officials across football, cricket, rugby union and rugby league in England. We know that the situation in England is challenging, precarious and untenable in the long term. We cannot continue on the current pathway, given the implications that any continuation will have on the sports examined in this book. Recruitment and retention of match officials involves challenging issues for governing bodies. Abuse towards these match officials can negatively contribute to dwindling recruitment numbers, increased drop out of current match officials, and detrimental impacts on the mental health and wellbeing of those who continue to officiate. If this situation is replicated in other countries, the concerns discussed in relation to England can be magnified and applied across Europe and other continents, leading to greater shortages in match official numbers, less fixtures taking place and fewer people taking part in sport and physical activity.

Therefore, it is important to examine both the reported incidents of abuse and the research which has been conducted in other sports and across different countries in order to ascertain whether there are broader trends related to the abuse of match officials, the support they receive from national and more localised associations and any subsequent reasons behind their discontinuation. Thus, this chapter focuses on the experiences of match officials in countries outside England through media reports outlining the current situation in different sports and different countries, alongside empirical research gathered in football in France and the Netherlands. The chapter, therefore, provides a synthesis of the current situation in which match officials operate, in order to better understand where, how and why the abuse occurs and, importantly, what we can learn in order to reduce this abuse.

Match officials in the media

There are frequent media reports regarding abuse directed towards match officials. At the elite level, match officials can be central to media reports, often following a perceived controversial incident during a high-profile fixture, or after a professed error or perceived misjudgement. These incidents can be portrayed as affecting the outcome of the fixture in question, with the resultant media reports often focusing on this decision making and the outcome of the decision on the fixture itself. The media reports can also consider the treatment of match officials by players, coaches and spectators, and these incidents are heavily publicised due to their pernicious nature.

Media stories can also focus on the lower levels of sport. However, when the focus shifts to these lower levels of sport the emphasis often revolves around the verbal and physical abuse towards match officials. These media reports demonstrate comparable trends in terms of the verbal and physical abuse directed towards match officials, and the sport in which the issues occur is often secondary in the evolving narrative. The focus in this chapter now turns to these media reports, the sports involved and also the country of origin of these reports.

Spectator behaviour

When considering spectator behaviour, many of the reports concentrate upon incidents in youth and grassroots sport. This is considered an issue, particularly with parents and the way that they behave on the side of the playing area. Wright (2019) identified that this poor or reduced adult spectator behaviour was affecting the number of match officials in sports, particularly high school football (soccer) in the United States (US). Indeed, the report entitled "Poor adult behavior reducing the number of willing referees" cites a referee who has assembled over 6,000 videos including examples of poor behaviour by people at sporting fixtures, even starting a Facebook page entitled "Offside", devoted to the gathering of information related to match official abuse. The article also states that there have been declining numbers of match officials nationally in the US, with nearly 80% of match officials discontinuing after their first two years, often citing aggressive parents as the reason (Wright, 2019).

A further report in the US also identified 80% of registered high school match officials discontinuing before they have completed three years according to the National Federation of State High School Associations. In North Carolina specifically, 70% of match officials do not continue after their first year in the role (Stump, 2018). From evidence like this, it is clear that the US has concerns about the number of match officials in football (soccer), with a widespread shortage of referees impacting the tri-state area of Kentucky, Illinois and Indiana, and the nation (Stratman, 2019). The availability of match officials has become a national crisis, with reports suggesting that it has the potential to change the landscape of youth sport, due to the reduced number of match officials in a variety of sports (Stump, 2018).

Another survey conducted by the National Association of Sports Officials in the US, comprising over 17,000 match officials across sports, found that 87% of respondents had suffered verbal abuse, 13% had been physically abused before or after a match and 57% of match officials believed that sportsmanship was getting worse (National Officiating Survey, 2017). Moreover, it is argued that in the US it is the youngest age groups in football (soccer) that are of the biggest concern in terms of abuse towards referees, with under 10 fixtures cited as the worst, and spectators as the specific issue (Froh, 2018). In 2015, John Bieniewicz, an amateur referee, was attacked and killed by a player and yet the problems still persist (Froh, 2018). There have also been recorded incidents in Canada, with both hockey and football (soccer) referees discontinuing. Approximately half of all new referees and umpires cease after their first year, and dropout rates have been as high as 60% across the match official population, as parents and coaches verbally abuse match officials, particularly at child or youth games (Mick, 2018).

It's not just spectators that are the problem

The shortage of referees has been blamed on the behaviour of parents, but also the behaviour of coaches and players. The Kentucky High School Athletic Association (KHSAA) stated that in 2018 they recruited and enlisted almost 4,000 licensed officials. However, in 2019 the number of licensed officials was reduced to 3,150, with the KHSAA believing that they need a greater number of referees, rather than numbers reducing.

The concerns regarding referee numbers in football (soccer) also extend to other sports in the US, such as the shortage of match officials in American Football in parts of the country. In Tulsa, Oklahoma, for example, issues in American Football are similar to those already identified in this book impacting upon football (soccer). It seems that the younger the children playing, the more poorly behaved the adults are who are watching the game (Associated Press, 2019). Incidents and issues leading to reduced numbers of match officials in American Football are also identified in other locations in the US, such as Alabama, Tennessee, Illinois, Missouri, California and Florida (Associated Press, 2019), in addition to Philadelphia and Massachusetts (Anastasia, 2019; Hohler, 2019). Furthermore, the National

Federation of State High School Associations (NFSHA) has attempted to address declining parent behaviour through the initiation of meetings to discuss concerns (Niehoff, 2019a), after identifying that older match officials were also discontinuing due to the negative behaviour of parents (Niehoff, 2019b).

The issues identified across the US also extend to female referees. In particular, reports suggest specific issues in high school football (soccer), with female referees recognising coaches and supporters as the perpetrators (Fitzgerald, 2019). To suggest that these incidents and concerns are reserved for the US, when considering these issues outside England would be disingenuous. For example, there are also media reports of problems recruiting female match officials across sports in Australia. Despite growing female sport participation numbers in Australia, this has not been matched by a similar increase in female match officials. Female match officials across football (soccer), cricket and rugby league are being held back by cultural barriers such as online abuse, sexism and lower pay, and match official numbers in these sports have been static, with umpire numbers in cricket actually deteriorating (SBS, 2019).

Moreover, there have been calls from match officials in Australia for the introduction of sin bins due to the rising level of dissent that all referees are experiencing in football (soccer) (Adno, 2019). It is feared that a lack of action will lead to football referees leaving the sport and the loss of 1,000 referees per year, something that is currently occurring, is not seen as sustainable (Adno, 2019). Indeed, Rugby Australia, the A-League and the Australian Football League (AFL) also identified issues with the turnover of match officials, specifically related to the prevalence of abuse (Barlass, 2019). The concerns currently being discussed have also been covered in academic literature, particularly considering Australian Rules football, umpire experiences and whether abuse was the predominant reason for discontinuation (Kellett & Shilbury, 2007; Kellett & Warner, 2011).

There have been demands for greater consideration of the challenges faced by sports match officials, particularly concerning the abuse to which they might be subjected. The abuse permeates all levels of sport, and in Australia the narrative has shifted towards harsher penalties for abuse and consideration of the mental health impacts, with rugby league and basketball officials asking for greater support to stop abuse and bullying during fixtures (Lloyd, 2018). Moreover, National Rugby League referee Matt Cecchin has spoken of the death threats and abuse that he receives during matches and also on social media as the primary reasons for leaving the sport (Cleary, 2018). The public nature of Cecchin's discontinuation has also led others involved in officiating in Australia to refer to a tipping point, with a high profile match official prepared to leave rugby league following the behaviour that he has experienced (Cleary, 2018). The National Rugby League also has identified that supporter abuse towards touch judges is a particular concern, with social media recognised as a particular issue (Walter, 2019). Threats towards a touch judge following a high-profile incident were instigated through social media channels (Walter, 2019) and the use of social media in abusive situations is beginning to attract academic attention (Kavanagh, Jones, & Sheppard-Marks, 2016).

Abuse from supporters, spectators and coaches has been identified as a specific issue related to the declining referee numbers in New Zealand. The Waikato football league in New Zealand reported a surge in abuse towards referees from coaches and other coaching related staff, as well as parents, meaning a deteriorating environment for football referees (Rowland, 2019). Also in New Zealand, reports have identified further issues with spectators and their behaviour towards match officials. Media reports from the Auckland area of New Zealand highlighted that a 15-year-old rugby union referee was punched and strangled by a spectator at a local under 12 age group fixture at which he was officiating. The incident occurred after the match had finished, with the spectator approaching the referee and following the altercation, having to be restrained by other spectators (Henry, 2019). This was the second report of a violent incident within a short space of time. The same report also outlined that a young rugby union referee was punched by an amateur player who had received a red card, with a 27-year-old man charged with assault over the incident (Henry, 2019). Cricket umpires are also not immune to some of these problems. For example, five cricket players in New Zealand were summoned to a judicial hearing after brawling and assaulting an umpire as part of the fracas, causing the match in question to be abandoned (Geenty & Fallon, 2019).

In South Africa, rugby union referees in Western Province agreed to strike in protest at the inadequate penalties for players, coaches and spectators guilty of verbal or physical abuse towards referees. Two particular incidents can be identified as the catalysts for this strike action: a referee being struck by a bottle thrown at him and verbal abuse from a coach towards another referee, both of which failed to invoke any retrospective action from the governing body (Dobson, 2019).

What about football specifically?

There have been numerous incidents of referee abuse in football, and these incidents are not necessarily country specific. We know that in England there have been strikes due to the level and amount of abuse that has been directed towards referees, with 2,000 referees going on strike in 2017 (Ames, 2017). Furthermore, in March 2019, referees in Jersey went on strike following a physical assault of a referee and the abuse and general poor behaviour of players, coaches and spectators (Pilnick, 2019). In the Republic of Ireland, verbal abuse has been described as a common occurrence (Malone, 2019), with physical assaults also evident in some cases (Keogh, 2018). Moreover, one referee in the Republic of Ireland was physically assaulted to such an extent that he had his jaw broken on both sides, another break higher up his jaw, a broken bone below his eye and stitches in his nose (Keogh, 2018).

The Football Association of Ireland has attempted to retain control of the situation by investigating incidents of reported assault upon referees. Since 2016, 15 separate cases of assault were investigated with punishments and bans given in 12 of the reported cases (Horgan-Jones, 2019). Three players have been banned for 40 years following the assault described in the previous paragraph, after which the referee had to undergo five hours of surgery and have plates inserted in his jaw. Furthermore, a referee who officiated school age football highlighted the amount and level of abuse he and his colleagues suffer on a weekly basis (Keville, 2019). The same referee stopped officiating in 2019 following an altercation with a coach, further abuse and a coach trying to strike him whilst he was refereeing, eventually stating that the environment was simply not safe enough to continue (Clarke, 2019).

In Germany, there have been an increasing number of attacks on referees. Despite 50,000 fewer matches played in the 2018/2019 season compared to the 2017/2018 season, a recent report from The German Football Association (DFB) identified a rise in the number of attacks (Attacks on referees on the rise in German amateur soccer leagues, 2019). In all, 2,906 verbal and physical attacks on referees were registered and reported during the 2018/2019 season, 40 more than the season before, with referees forced to abandon 685 games due to violence or discrimination (Attacks on referees on the rise in German amateur soccer leagues, 2019). There have also been problems in specific regions of Germany. In Cologne, for example, during a match between Blau-Weiss Köln and Germania Ossendorf on 3 November 2019, a referee was verbally abused and physically attacked by members of the away team and also had a glass bottle thrown at him after awarding three goals to Blau-Weiss Köln (Martyr, 2019).

In Switzerland, there have also been incidents of referee abuse. One such episode involved an amateur footballer being banned for 50 years after kicking a ball in the referee's face and then spraying the referee with water (Orr, 2014). There have also been incidents so difficult to control that riot police had to be called onto the pitch. In Peru a cup fixture between Deportivo Garcilaso and Deportivo Llacuabamba descended into violence, requiring the riot police to enter the field of play in order to protect the referee and his assistants after they were attacked by spectators (Valdez, 2019).

A tragic incident in the Netherlands led to increased scrutiny of the support and provision for referees. In 2012 an assistant referee, Richard

Nieuwenhuizen, who was volunteering at his son's youth football match as an assistant referee (linesperson), collapsed and died several hours after being punched and kicked by a number of players (Mohamed, 2013). Six amateur footballers and the father of one of the players were subsequently convicted of manslaughter, whilst a silent march in his memory comprising of more than 12,000 people took place in Almere on 9 December 2012 (Mohamed, 2013). In Mexico, a referee was carried from the pitch unconscious, and later died from a traumatic brain injury after being attacked and assaulted by a player on the pitch after being given a red card (Soccer referee dies after assault by player, 2018). The death of referees has also been evident in other countries. For example, a referee was shot dead and an opposition player wounded by a footballer during an amateur match in Argentina, after he had shown the player a red card (Gibson, 2016).

The extent of the coverage of these incidents, aligned with their exposure across sports and countries, demonstrates the widescale nature of this problem outside England. However, little is known as to the underlying causes, long-term impacts and the efficacy of governing body responses of these incidents. Whilst there has been some academic research conducted in other countries (see for example Livingston, Forbes, Wattie, & Cunningham, 2020), this research is sparse and requires updating and developing further, particularly given the incidents outlined.

Football referees in France and the Netherlands

In beginning to address this gap in the literature, we present here survey research conducted with football referees in France and the Netherlands. We compare the findings with the current evidence in England. The comparison of referee responses in France and the Netherlands provides the ability to consider any trends from the data and further explore some of the issues and areas raised by referees. In doing so, an online survey was constructed that received 3,408 responses from referees in France and 1,229 from referees in the Netherlands. To compare the situation across both countries with England, part of the survey asked the referees whether they had been subjected to any form of verbal abuse (see Figure 6.1).

Although a significant number of referees in France reported that they had received some form of verbal abuse (68.1%) and over half of the responses from referees in the Netherlands also reported verbal abuse (51%), these figures are more comparable with rugby union (53.7%) and cricket (56.5%) in England, rather than football (93.7%) or rugby league (85.4%). When the referees were asked about incidents of physical abuse, the figures were more comparable to those found in football and rugby league in England (see Figure 6.2).

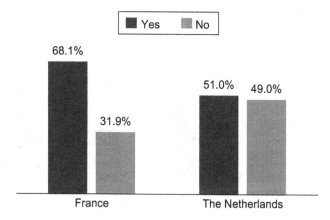

Figure 6.1 Have you been verbally abused?

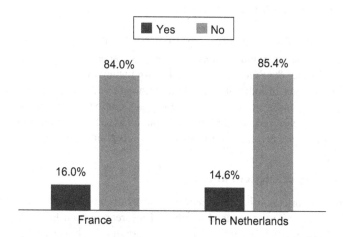

Figure 6.2 Have you been physically abused?

As outlined in Figure 6.2, referees in both France and the Netherlands reported similar levels of physical abuse, figures which were comparable to those in football (18.9%) in England (Cleland, Webb, & O'Gorman, 2018) and rugby league (16.9%) in England (Webb, Rayner, & Thelwell, 2018). However, it is the frequency of the abuse that demonstrates the greatest difference across the countries in football (see Figure 6.3).

We can see from the referee responses that the frequency of the abuse to which referees are subjected is 14.4% for at least every couple of games in France and 2.2% for at least every couple of games in the Netherlands. As

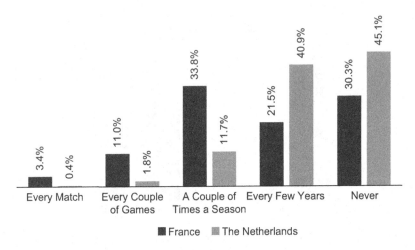

Figure 6.3 How often do you receive what you would consider to be abuse?

we reported in Chapter 2, this compares to 59.7% of referees in England that reported abuse every match or every couple of games (Cleland et al., 2018; Webb, Cleland, & O'Gorman, 2017). The frequency of the abuse appears to be much greater in football in England, although when we start to analyse the open responses from referees, we can see comparable trends in terms of the subjects raised and commented upon. These trends are also evident across sports and are explored further in the subsequent section.

Referee experiences of abuse

Referees reported similar experiences in terms of their exposure to abusive incidents. Despite the reduced number of referees in both France and the Netherlands reporting that they had been verbally or physically abused at some point in their career, there were still over 50% in both countries who had experienced abuse. This was reflected in the illustrative responses from the referees, who expanded upon some of the abuse to which they had been subjected.

One referee from the Netherlands (male, 21+ years' experience, 55–64 age group) explained how severely he was physically assaulted on one occasion, and that the person who committed the assault was subsequently banned for a period of time:

> I was knocked unconscious by a player. I did not report this, but the Koninklijke Nederlandse Voetbal Bond (KNVB) acted immediately

after rumours about the incident and suspended the perpetrator for 7 years and removed the team from the competition for a number of years.

The response from the governing body, the KNVB, was well received by this referee, and it could be that the tragedy of the incident involving Richard Nieuwenhuizen in 2012 has led to a refocus of policy, and a reduced level of tolerance for abuse towards match officials. However, another referee (male, 21+ years' experience, 65+ age group) illustrated that the situation is becoming worse and has definitely declined since he started officiating in the 1960s: "I started as a referee in 1963, but after all I know I would not start again. Acceptance of referee decisions has decreased for me".

In France, the illustration of abusive incidents was stark, with one example evidencing how much danger referees and the general public can be in when problems begin to occur:

> I wrote a report, but the sanction was not severe enough. The player intentionally injured a player, tried to kick the injured man, punched an opponent, insulted and showed his fists to the referee, stole the scoresheet and licenses, brought six of his friends onto the field, and blocked the exit of the parking lot with his friends (armed with knives). He only got a 24 game suspension. In my opinion he should have been excluded for several years by the disciplinary committee.
>
> (Male, 3–5 years' experience, 35–44 age group)

Clearly the situation escalated following incidents that occurred on the field of play. The conditions were extremely dangerous once the friends of the player in question came onto the pitch, and then blocked the car park exit. Another referee (male, 21+ years' experience, 45–54 age group) amongst many examples, outlined their experiences and the regularity with which they are abused in France: "We are assaulted by spectators verbally, and regularly threatened. It would be essential to make clubs aware of their responsibilities for security in stadiums or around pitches and any issues or transgressions should be punished more severely". The severity of the punishment in both of these cases has been identified by the referees as an issue. Moreover, this situation has also led to referees in France asking for players and clubs to be monitored much more closely than is currently the case, as illustrated by this referee: "The sanctions on a player should be much more severe, because it is often the same players who are aggressive and who ruin your match" (male, 16–20 years' experience, 35–44 age group). Some referees identified the players as the problem, whereas other referees (male, 3–5 years' experience, 55–64 age group) observed that it is also the clubs that require further sanctions, not just the players, and that monitoring of these problem clubs should be much more widespread than is currently the case: "Regarding assaults, more regular monitoring of the clubs concerned, because they are always the same. Heavier penalties when the facts are proven".

These abusive situations naturally required the support of the governing bodies, and any monitoring of players or clubs also requires support and organisation from those same governing bodies. In England issues were identified with support across the different sports, and the communication between the governing bodies and the referees in matters related to disciplinary procedures (see Chapter 3).

Support and disciplinary processes

There are similar concerns with the support and disciplinary processes expressed by referees in France and the Netherlands, to those matters communicated by match officials in Chapter 3. Match officials identified a lack of support across sports in England, and in the Netherlands referees wanted the KNVB to be more facilitative. One referee (male, 11–15 years' experience, 25–34 age group) believed that the KNVB need to be more approachable, particularly in regional or local areas: "Better involvement from the KNVB. This means more approachable, more people at district offices. Make sure that the structure within the KNVB is in order. This also has an impact on the referees". This referee and many others believed that the structure around match officials is important, and this support can mean that match officials are retained in sport, rather than opting to leave (as we expressed in Chapter 4). This is particularly true for new or young referees. The media reports illustrated earlier in this chapter have outlined the dropout rates of young match officials, in the US particularly, with nearly 80% of match officials discontinuing after their first two years (Wright, 2019). Therefore, the support and guidance for these new referees is essential, with this referee (male, 6–10 years' experience, 45–54 age group) explaining that this period of support should be longer, and additional support should be provided for referees who have suffered abuse:

> For new referees we need a longer period of guidance. For referees who have had to deal with violence, provide a supervisor, certainly for a period of 1 to 2 months to support the referee concerned. Then ensure that this guidance is on standby when the referee asks for it.

The continuing support after an incident of abuse is cited as something which should be available, should the match official require it. In France, this support is something that referees believed is in short supply. This referee (male, 16–20 years' experience, 35–44 age group) believed that the situation in lower league football evidences a lack of support: "What is happening in amateur football is scandalous. The referees are almost left to their own devices". The identification of referees being isolated and how any abuse towards these referees might negatively affect them led another referee (male, 3–5 years' experience, 25–34 age group) to explain that players should have to officiate at some point during the season, so that they understand the role of the referee and the challenges that they face: "I think that at the district level, a day or two of the championship should be refereed entirely by players . . . they realise the impact their outrageous attitude can have and the difficulty for the referees to be constantly challenged".

Developing a better understanding for players of the role of the referee could help with the way that they behave towards the referee during a match. It is when the support around referees or match officials is perceived to deteriorate that issues begin to occur. Another referee in France (male, 21+ years' experience, 55–64 age group) explained that he saw a young referee being assaulted during a game by the president of a club who later assaulted the referee in a disciplinary hearing. This altercation also involved the police and the referees association:

> There is no support. I witnessed the assault of a young colleague on the field by a club president for the first time last season and this same aggressor punched me in a disciplinary committee before a dozen officials. I complained to the police, my referees association supported me by putting a lawyer at my disposal immediately and free of charge. The case is continuing.

Clearly clubs, and individuals involved in the organisation and management of clubs, being involved in aggressive behaviour towards referees is concerning. The support in this case appears to have been strong from the referees association, although the incidents that are occurring led another referee (male, 16–20 years' experience, 25–34 age group), by way of illustration, to argue that cameras are required around football grounds, principally for the safety of the referee and to identify any individuals who are physically abusive: "We need cameras in stadiums as well as in the hallways of the locker rooms. I think it's feasible and it would deter so many teams who hide behind the fact that they are not the attackers or they do not know the attackers". This would be expensive to instigate, but it would help to identify the individuals who are guilty of these actions. This would also make sanctions easier to initiate, with another referee (male, less than 2 years' experience, 25–34 age group) from France stating that sanctions are important, as is the aftercare for referees who have been subjected to abuse: "Sanctions against the bigger culprits [are needed]. I suggest some meetings with a psychologist and with several referees who are victims of aggression".

Support after an incident was also deemed important by referees, who paid particular attention to support during the disciplinary process. We know that in England the disciplinary process was an issue across sports (as considered in Chapter 3 through the non-reporting of incidents). This experience is something upon which referees in both France and the Netherlands also commented. For example, in the Netherlands comments regarding the KNVB often revolved around the slow or burdensome nature of the reporting process for referees, rather than a complete lack of support from the governing body. One referee (male, 21+ years' experience, 45–54 age group) identified a potential solution through the construction of a platform to share complaints about clubs, or how referees are received or supported once they arrive at a club:

> A platform or site where you can easily share complaints, bad experiences or good experiences. E.g., poor reception at a club or unpleasant encounters due to situations on the field, you often let this go because it is all too cumbersome to report to the KNVB (not worth the effort).

The fact that this referee believed the system was too onerous and therefore it was "not worth the effort" to report some of the incidents, corresponds with the comments in England and the lack of reporting in some cases. Referees reported similar concerns in France, although they were more insistent about revisions to the disciplinary process and the disciplinary committee. An illustrative example from a referee in France (male, 6–10 years' experience, 18–24 age group) demonstrates the strength of feeling from referees and the lack of support they feel during a disciplinary procedure: "Change of function in the discipline commissions, because the referee often finds himself alone to defend himself [at the commission hearing] surrounded by those accusing him and all the rest of the club's players wanting to defend them too". This isolation in the disciplinary process and the hearing itself is concerning, particularly if this involves young referees. This situation would be daunting for any referee or match official, but even more so for a young referee who might have to testify against an individual who has recently verbally or physically abused them.

The influence of professional football

Referees from France and the Netherlands recognised the impact of both Ligue 1 in France and the Eredivisie in the Netherlands on those referees operating at local or regional levels. Certainly, as with examples in England discussed in Chapter 5, referees in both countries identified correlations between negative incidents occurring in their top professional divisions, and the subsequent behaviour of players in local leagues and competitions over the following weeks. In the Netherlands referees believed that the behaviour of the referees in the Eredivisie, as well as the players, leads to problems for referees in lower league football. One referee (male, 21+ years' experience, 35–44 age group) argued that referees in the Eredivisie need to be stricter with players who deserve to be punished: "Referees in professional football do not dare to give cards to players who ask for cards, or deserve cards, and with words or gestures disagree with the referee. The amateurs copy that". The belief that the amateurs copy the behaviour of professional players is also a subject which was raised by other referees, illustrated by this referee in the Netherlands (male, 3–5 years' experience, 45–54 age group), who believed that the Eredivisie should be setting an example, similar to that in other sports:

> We need example behaviour in the Premier Division (Eredivisie). This is copied on the field of play lower down. Take a look at rugby and hockey. Totally different behaviour in the premier division and you can also see this on the field. This just doesn't make sense and makes work much harder for referees.

The link between the professional game and behaviour in the amateur game is difficult to authenticate. Nevertheless, if referees who operate at those levels believe that there is a link, they are in the best position to judge whether there is a relationship between the professional game and incidents at amateur level. Another referee in the Netherlands (male, 16–20 years' experience, 55–64 age group) believed that the media coverage of the professional game does not help referees with their analysis and critique of referee decisions: "It starts at the highest level with the media 'analysing' and criticising every decision a top referee makes. This all filters down to grassroots level".

This link between the professional game and the amateur game was also commented upon by referees in France. Referees even believed that the referees operating in Ligue 1 should be sanctioned if they do not apply the laws of the game correctly, with the example given of players crowding around the referee following a decision, exemplified by this referee (male, 11–15 years' experience, 45–54 age group):

> There should be greater responsibility and sanctions for elite referees. When we see the professional players crowd around the referee

following a decision . . . . this remains intolerable at this level, and the repercussions are immediate at the lower levels.

The replication and imitation of behaviour is something which referees in France also believed subsequently impacted upon them at lower levels. Another referee (male, 21+ years' experience, 45–54 age group) illustrated that referees at lower levels will continue to be challenged if this behaviour is allowed to continue in the professional game. In particular, the referee, representing a number of similar responses from the data, believed that there should be commissions that operate after the match, utilising existing footage and dealing with players that they believe are guilty of misconduct:

> It is complicated for a league level or district level referee not to be challenged, when he sees on TV referees being surrounded by several players as soon as a decision is made. The professional match referee cannot give five or six warnings at once to all players. A commission could do this afterwards using existing images, without the need for an additional camera. This would, in my opinion, have a beneficial effect on all football, professional and amateur.

If it can be argued that authorities and those in positions of governance are dealing with these issues in the professional game, referees believed that the current approach is not working. Referees in both countries acknowledged that negative behaviour in the professional leagues can and does impact upon those referees operating at lower levels of the game, and in turn, makes their job much more difficult. But there is no easy solution. The elite leagues in each country are the subject of significant media deals and television revenue (Webb, 2017), and as such the mass dismissal of players is not something that would be well supported by the leagues, particularly if the action then diminished the spectacle of the league. However, referees also believed that the current situation is negatively affecting them, and therefore some sort of solution should be sought. In addressing this, we consider some potential solutions and policy implications in the concluding chapter of this book.

Conclusion

This chapter began by examining the media coverage of match official abuse across the world. These reports suggested some of the reasons for the shortages of match officials, alongside a high dropout rate, particularly concerning match officials who are relatively newly qualified. Some of this discontinuation is due to the abuse to which these match officials are subjected. Negative incidents present a very real and important risk to the wellbeing and mental health of the match officials who receive verbal or physical abuse (as discussed in Chapter 5). The media reports covered in this chapter are those that have received the most attention, and often these incidents are the most shocking. However, for all of these higher profile incidents, there are thousands of other cases of abuse occurring on a regular basis in countries and sports across the world that are not covered by the media. In many cases, the abusive incidents are either not reported (see Chapter 3) or the match officials struggle to understand or trust the disciplinary processes or are not satisfied with the communication from those in positions of governance following the reporting of an incident of abuse.

This chapter has also considered what is happening in football in both France and the Netherlands. Interestingly, there are a number of trends that are evident in France and the Netherlands which have been explored in earlier chapters in England across sports. Most noticeably, the issues with abuse, the disciplinary system and also the link between the professional game and the lower levels of football are areas which evidence these trends. Clearly there are also differences between sports and also countries, and we should not underrepresent the value of cultural difference as a part of this, but, likewise, we also should not dismiss the trends that are evident either.

Nevertheless, it is important as we reach the final chapter of this book to consider the implications of the findings discussed across the first six chapters. The final chapter (Chapter 7) focuses on policy implications and potential solutions to some of the issues that this book has raised. Furthermore, areas of good practice have been identified in order to start to move towards a more joined up approach between sports. In addressing some of the emergent trends, evident in different countries and in different sports as we have seen in this chapter, the intention is to improve the status quo for match officials and the wider sporting environment for all participants.

References

Adno, C. (2019). *Referee Kris Griffiths-Jones wants to see the introduction of sin bins for dissent.* Retrieved from www.foxsports.com.au/football/a-league/referee-kris-griffithsjones-wants-to-see-the-introduction-of-sin-bins-for-dissent/news-story/75e0b558f0f14bb3328d211e9bc15677

Ames, N. (2017). *"More than 2,000" referees on strike lead to grassroots postponements.* Retrieved from www.theguardian.com/football/2017/mar/05/referees-on-strike-grassroots-postponements

Anastasia, P. (2019). *Referee shortage: It's a big problem for high school and youth sports that is getting worse.* Retrieved from www.inquirer.com/high-school-sports/pennsylvania/official-shortage-referee-high-school-youth-sports-southeastern-pennsylvania-south-jersey-20191101.html

Associated Press. (2019). Retrieved from www.fox32chicago.com/sports/referees-quitting-at-record-rate-because-of-abuse-from-parents-players-and-coaches

Attacks on referees on the rise in German amateur soccer leagues. (2019). Retrieved from www.dw.com/en/attacks-on-referees-on-the-rise-in-german-amateur-soccer-leagues/a-49530305

Barlass, T. (2019). *Referee abuse drives high turnover rate among junior sports officials.* Retrieved from www.smh.com.au/national/referee-abuse-drives-high-turnover-rate-among-junior-sports-officials-20190522-p51q4a.html

Clarke, H. (2019). *"Today I had a manager attempt to strike me": Young referee quits and hits out at FAI.* Retrieved from www.independent.ie/sport/soccer/today-i-had-a-manager-attempt-to-strike-me-young-referee-quits-and-hits-out-at-fai-38244757.html

Cleary, M. (2018). *Referees reach tipping point after revelations about death threats.* Retrieved from www.theguardian.com/sport/2018/aug/04/referees-reach-tipping-point-after-revelations-about-death-threats

Cleland, J., O'Gorman, J., & Webb, T. (2018). Respect? An investigation into the experience of referees in association football. *The International Review for the Sociology of Sport, 53*(8), 960–974. doi: 10.1177/1012690216687979

Dobson, P. (2019). *WP referees go on strike over abuse.* Retrieved from https://rugby365.com/laws-referees/news/whistles-grow-silent-in-wp

Fitzgerald, M. (2019). *Why I stopped officiating high school soccer.* Retrieved from www.bostonglobe.com/sports/high-schools/2019/11/01/why-stopped-officiating-high-school-soccer/KsssTEkzEApi8SsWtVxelN/story.html?camp=bg:brief:rss:feedly&rss_id=feedly_rss_brief&s_campaign=bostonglobe:socialflow:twitter

Froh, T. (2018). *"My under-10 matches are the worst": No end in sight to youth referee abuse.* Retrieved from www.theguardian.com/sport/2018/apr/16/my-under-10-matches-are-the-worst-no-end-in-sight-to-youth-referee-abuse

Geenty, M., & Fallon, V. (2019). *Judicial hearing to decide fate of five brawling cricketers as police say no charges laid.* Retrieved from www.stuff.co.nz/sport/cricket/110691547/judicial-hearing-to-decide-fate-of-brawling-cricketers-as-police-say-no-charges-laid

Gibson, S. (2016). *Match abandoned in Argentina hen red-carded player returns with gun and shoots referee and opposition player.* Retrieved from www.telegraph.co.uk/sport/football/12159807/Match-abandoned-in-Argentina-when-red-carded-player-returns-with-gun-and-shoots-referee-and-opposition-player.html

Henry, D. (2019). *Young ref "punched, strangled" by spectator after under-12s rugby game.* Retrieved from www.nzherald.co.nz/nz/news/article.cfm?c_id=1&objectid=12254068

Hohler, B. (2019). *There's a shortage of high school game officials in Massachusetts, and abusive fans are at fault.* Retrieved from www.bostonglobe.com/sports/high-schools/2019/11/01/official-referee-shortage-massachuetts-high-schools-miaa/Qdv0UMlQ8fYkhhhgDbzDvI/story.html?p1=Article_Inline_Text_Link

Horgan-Jones, J. (2019). *FAI hands out punishments for 12 alleged assaults on match officials.* Retrieved from www.irishtimes.com/news/ireland/irish-news/fai-hands-out-punishments-for-12-alleged-assaults-on-match-officials-1.3936356

Kavanagh, E., Jones, I., & Sheppard-Marks, L. (2016). Towards typologies of virtual maltreatment: Sport, digital cultures & dark leisure. *Leisure Studies, 5*(6), 783–96. doi: 10.1080/02614367.2016.1216581

Kellett, P., & Shilbury, D. (2007). Umpire participation: Is abuse really the issue? *Sport Management Review, 10*(3), 209–229. doi: 10.1016/S1441-3523(07)70012-8

Kellett, P., & Warner, S. (2011). Creating communities that lead to retention: The social worlds and communities of umpires. *European Sport Management Quarterly, 11*(5), 471–494. doi: 10.1080/16184742.2011.624109

Keogh, F. (2018). *Referee's jaw broken after attack in Irish amateur league.* Retrieved from www.bbc.co.uk/sport/football/46180452

Keville, G. (2019). *"Two spectators wanted to fight me in the carpark": Young schoolboy referee highlights "toxic" abuse he receives.* Retrieved from www.independent.ie/sport/soccer/two-spectators-wanted-to-fight-me-in-the-carpark-young-schoolboy-referee-highlights-toxic-abuse-he-receives-37970516.html

Livingston, L., Forbes, S. L., Wattie, N., & Cunningham, I. (2020). *Sports officiating: Recruitment, development and retention.* London: Routledge.

Lloyd, S. (2018). *Bullying, abuse of referees prompts call for mental health support of sporting officials.* Retrieved from www.abc.net.au/news/2018-09-22/referee-bullying-call-mental-health-support-officials/10281392

Malone, E. (2019). *Refereeing not for the faint-hearted or sensitive.* Retrieved from www.irishtimes.com/sport/soccer/refereeing-not-for-the-faint-hearted-or-sensitive-1.4076970

Martyr, K. (2019). *German football referees strike over player violence.* Retrieved from www.dw.com/en/german-football-referees-strike-over-player-violence/a-51287190

Mick, H. (2018). *A shortage of young referees due to abuse from parents and coaches.* Retrieved from www.theglobeandmail.com/life/parenting/a-shortage-of-young-referees-due-to-abuse-from-parents-and-coaches/article570900/

Mohamed, M. (2013). *Richard Nieuwenhuizen death: Six teenagers and 50-year-old father convicted of manslaughter in shocking case of referee killed over a game of football.* Retrieved from www.independent.co.uk/news/world/europe/richard-nieuwenhuizen-death-six-teenagers-and-50-year-old-father-convicted-of-manslaughter-in-8662177.html

National Officiating Survey. (2017). *17,487 officials had something to say.* Retrieved from www.naso.org/survey/

Niehoff, K. (2019a). *The NFHS voice: Respect for everyone in high school sports and activities.* Retrieved from www.nfhs.org/articles/the-nfhs-voice-respect-for-everyone-in-high-school-sports-and-activities/

Niehoff, K. (2019b). *The NFHS voice: Veteran officials "hanging it up" because of unruly behavior by parents.* Retrieved from www.nfhs.org/articles/the-nfhs-voice-veteran-officials-hanging-it-up-because-of-unruly-behavior-by-parents/

Orr, J. (2014). *Footballer receives astonishing 50-year ban for booting the ball in the referee's face and spraying him with water.* Retrieved from www.independent.co.uk/

sport/football/news-and-comment/footballer-receives-astonishing-50-year-ban-for-attacking-referee-9834205.html

Pilnick, B. (2019). *Jersey referees to strike over bad behaviour.* Retrieved from www.bbc.co.uk/sport/football/47720839

Rowland, T. (2019). *Waikato football league cracks down on abuse from the sidelines and on the field.* Retrieved from www.nzherald.co.nz/hamilton-news/sport/news/article.cfm?c_id=1503364&objectid=12251153

SBS. (2019). Retrieved from www.sbs.com.au/news/nothing-will-change-more-is-needed-to-boost-australian-women-s-referee-numbers

Soccer referee dies after assault by player. (2018). Retrieved from https://mexiconewsdaily.com/news/soccer-referee-dies-after-assault-by-player/

Stratman, J. (2019). *Referee shortage continues in the Tri-State.* Retrieved from www.14news.com/2019/09/30/referee-shortage-continues-tri-state/

Stump, S. (2018). *Youth sports referees across the US are quitting because of abusive parents.* Retrieved from www.today.com/parents/youth-sports-referees-across-us-are-quitting-because-abusive-parents-t126087

Valdez, C. (2019). *Soccer pitch or battlefield? Peru Cup game turns ugly.* Retrieved from https://sports.yahoo.com/soccer-pitch-battlefield-peru-cup-233731686.html?src=rss&guccounter=1&guce_referrer=aHR0cHM6Ly93d3cuZ29vZ2xlLmNvbS8&guce_referrer_sig=AQAAAHeilQPb0w5vBOvjwKBMVw_EA0Rn_dWL69WrECVQH1O0XxI094Mt49IlfTTdMtGVSSGL5zUcS_6d2juHWg8kmkxwVVMkJ9rMxbHBJAKHgRAihRnaOe4MAs_Gz9oDeXU_HaMuiVwBu-NnzzVNPRfCmWM5h0BJ_m9DYmEKeXV1kWhR

Walter, B. (2019). *NRL calls for end to touch judge abuse over Vunivalu error.* Retrieved from www.nrl.com/news/2019/09/16/nrl-calls-for-end-to-touch-judge-abuse-over-vunivalu-error/

Webb, T. (2017). *Elite soccer referees: Officiating in the Premier League, La Liga and Serie A.* London: Routledge.

Webb, T., Cleland, J., & O'Gorman, J. (2017). The distribution of power through a media campaign: The respect programme, referees and violence in association football. *The Journal of Global Sport Management, 2*(3), 162–181. doi: 10.1080/24704067.2017.1350591

Webb, T., Rayner, M., & Thelwell, R. (2018). An explorative case study of referee abuse in English Rugby League. *Journal of Applied Sport Management, 10*(2). doi: 10.18666/JASM-2017-V10-12-8834

Wright, S. (2019). *Poor adult behavior reducing the number of willing referees.* Retrieved from www.ksfy.com/content/news/Poor-adult-behavior-reducing-the-number-of-willing-referees-559896621.html

7 Evidencing good practice and tackling abuse

Through the voices of 8,010 match officials, this book has addressed a wide variety of issues covering the level of formal and informal support, abuse and experiences encountered as part of their role as an independent arbiter of rules and laws across sports and countries. The implications of the abuse have been considered in detail from the perspective of individual match officials, often focused on the potential consequences for different sports if abuse remains unchallenged (see Chapter 5). However, it is important as this book comes to a close, to focus upon the techniques and methods that can be utilised to challenge abuse in the future.

Without any form of action from governing bodies, leagues and organisations that support, train and develop match officials, the status quo will remain. Match officials will continue to be verbally and physically abused, leading to discontinuation and more fixtures continuing without match officials, or being cancelled completely. Moreover, in order to increase their investment and structures around match officials, governing bodies also need to consider the format of any formal and informal support networks and disciplinary processes within which match officials need to feel secure.

Therefore, this chapter includes a considered focus detailing examples of good practice from different sports around the world in terms of supporting their match officials and tackling the issues identified in this book, mostly pertaining to the level of abuse and support they receive. At the heart of this chapter is a 10-point plan we have developed to control and reduce abuse, increase support and improve retention of match officials in sport, as well as improve the sporting environment for all stakeholders. This plan has been developed as a result of the extensive research that has been conducted and is presented in this book. It is hoped that this plan and directed approach will provide opportunities for governing bodies, leagues and match official organisations to reflect on the treatment of their match officials and consider what they are doing well and what factors could be improved. This will also help to address the requirement for the increased recruitment of match officials in a number of sports and countries and begin to tackle the discontinuation of match officials.

Good practice and innovations in match official support in England

This book has identified numerous concerns related to the abuse of match officials. These issues require attention from those in positions of governance in order to address some of the problems around abuse and support enabling better retention of match officials (see Chapter 3). However, it is also the case that sports governing bodies are focusing on these matters and are actively pursuing methods to improve the working environment for match officials. Some sports governing bodies have witnessed the problems associated with the abuse of match officials and have decided to act to address this toxic culture of abuse, predominantly perpetrated by players, coaches and spectators. In order to do this, a number of innovations and policy initiatives have been launched in different sports and countries. We focus on some of these initiatives in the following as a means of providing guidance to governing bodies and administrators involved in the leadership and management of match officials, as well as match officials themselves.

We have already considered the launch, impact and thoughts related to the Respect Programme in football in England (see Chapter 2). This initiative has instigated some fundamental changes to the structures of football, particularly at the youth and grassroots level, although the perceptions of the programme have been mixed from the referee workforce (Cleland, O'Gorman, & Bond, 2015; Cleland, O'Gorman, & Webb, 2018; Webb, Cleland, & O'Gorman, 2017). Nevertheless, the FA in England have also attempted to tackle the behaviour of players, and their language towards referees, through the introduction of temporary dismissals, or sin bins as they have become known. These sin bins are designed to tackle inappropriate behaviour in youth and grassroots football and have provided referees with the power to send players from the field of play for 10 minutes as a punishment for dissent (The FA, 2019a). Sin bins were first trialled in the 2017–18 and 2018–19 seasons and then brought into force at all levels of grassroots football including mini soccer and youth leagues and adult amateur football, as well those including veterans and disabled players. The FA released information stating that 25 of the 31 trial leagues involved showed a 38% reduction in dissent across all leagues. Moreover, 72% of players, 77% of managers/coaches and 84% of referees wanted the initiative to continue after the trial phase had ended (The FA, 2019a; Rathborn, 2019).

Some County FAs in English football have also begun to focus on the reduction of abuse towards their referees. Dorset County FA, for example, has initiated a scheme whereby under 18 referees all wear a yellow arm band. Coaches and spectators particularly, are alerted to the fact that the referee or assistant referee is under 18. This means that coaches and spectators are therefore subject to child safeguarding measures and match day responsibilities operating with minors. Other County FAs have also launched schemes whereby referees under 18 wear armbands, with Cheshire FA, Essex FA, Hampshire FA and Staffordshire FA all subscribing to a similar approach to help identify and support their younger referees.

In order to further support young referees, as well as referees of other ages, match day observers have been introduced in Dorset, England. These observers are there to monitor behaviour and to report on any incidents that they believe are negatively impacting upon referees and the wider game, as one referee (male, 3–5 years' experience, 25–34 age group) explains:

> Match day observers go out and watch games, including games with adult referees and under18 referees. Their role is to watch the game, referee, players and managers' behaviour, to report anything that has been missed by the referee. Sometimes these match day observers go incognito, sometimes they make themselves known.

The role of the match day observer is varied, although part of this remit appears to be to act as an independent support mechanism for referees, particularly if there is negative behaviour outside of the pitch area that the referee might miss when they are on the pitch. The support around match officials is essential (Ridinger, Kim, Warner, & Tingle, 2017a; Ridinger, Warner, Tingle, & Kim, 2017b) and this support network is particularly vital for young referees, given their vulnerability as minors and also the fact that governing bodies are trying to retain a greater number of match officials (see Chapter 3). There are also examples of schemes and initiatives that are instigated by the match officials themselves, rather than the governing body or referee societies. Referees affiliated to Dorset FA, for example, have taken it upon themselves to provide further support for other referees who might experience difficulties or problems during a match or following a match. Referees have set up a scheme called the 'listening ear', as explained by one referee (male, 3–5 years' experience, 25–34 age group):

> We have a scheme that was setup recently by several senior referees, which is called the listening ear. This is for anyone who feels like they are struggling, or have had a tough day at the office, where they can ring or text these people who will provide a listening ear and help or advice

on what happened. I'm involved in this, we have a couple of teachers, a former nurse who worked in mental health and a couple of others.

The 'listening ear' scheme provides a service for referees who might experience issues during a match. These issues can be abuse-related, difficulties with one particular game, player or team or merely for advice on aspects of their performance or training. This type of scheme is not mandatory, and it is also not something that is replicated in every County FA. There are other organisations that can provide similar services, such as the charitable organisation RefSupport in England which has a dedicated phoneline for referees, predominantly designed to provide support on a national scale (RefSupport, n.d.). The existence of an independent organisation such as RefSupport suggests some evident gaps in the provision of support for referees in football and raises questions regarding the role and function of County FAs, in particular, moving forwards.

Good practice and innovations in match official support around the world

There are also other examples of phonelines that have been introduced as a measure of additional support for match officials. The KNVB in the Netherlands has introduced a phoneline, designed to be utilised by referees should they experience abuse on the field of play. To provide the service the KNVB has partnered with 24/7, an organisation that specialises in aftercare for traumatic experiences. The phoneline is operational 24 hours a day and is designed to support those referees who suffer a shocking event, such as:

- A physical threat or confrontation with physical injury due to violence or aggression.
- An impaired physical or mental condition as a result of violence or aggression.
- Death as a result of violence or aggression.
- Terror, disbelief, bewilderment and intense powerlessness.
- (Death) anxiety, physical (stress) reactions, apathy and numbness.

(KNVB, n.d.a)

In addition, an assessment is made to ascertain what, if any, support the referee requires and what aftercare should be provided. This aftercare involves supporting the referee following the incident, with each individual referee and case treated individually.

The KNVB have also launched a violence prevention initiative, in partnership with the organisation Halt. Halt works to predominantly combat juvenile delinquency and targets youth football players who are given bans over violent attacks. The young players are offered behavioural training, with attendance and engagement incentivised by the fact that if the programme of training is successfully completed, the young players can have their suspensions reduced (KNVB, n.d.b). The negative behaviour of the young players can be towards another player or a referee, but Halt and the KNVB work with the clubs to provide safety advice and tips as well as behavioural interventions, such as Aggression Regulation Training (ART), group based approaches, recovery and meditation processes, and sport and behaviour processes (KNVB, n.d.b). All of these interventions and approaches are designed to improve the playing environment for players, referees and spectators and to address any underlying behavioural concerns with young players (see Chapter 4 for further information).

In other countries outside Europe there are examples of extended support for match officials, with the governing body often taking a lead role in these initiatives. In Australia, Hockey Australian Capital Territory (ACT) has launched a number of initiatives designed to promote the role and support their umpires in hockey. In 2013 Hockey ACT introduced a "season of respect" which was targeted toward reducing abuse of umpires, promoting fair play and raising awareness of appropriate behaviour (Hockey ACT Umpire Handbook, 2013). An associated initiative, "play the whistle" designed to identify junior teams that behave in a positive manner, was also introduced as part of the "season of respect". "Play the whistle" encouraged players, coaches, spectators and officials to play in the spirit of the game, with umpires marking each team related to their behaviour after every fixture (Hockey ACT Umpire Handbook, 2013).

More recently Hockey New South Wales (NSW) ran a junior umpire programme designed to provide a safe learning environment for the umpires. The programme aims to empower the mentors/umpire coaches through training and education, to take action against any coaches, spectators or players who are abusing umpires. Moreover, alongside this programme Hockey NSW also launched a "take the pledge" campaign. The campaign encouraged players, teams, spectators and clubs to champion the respect of umpires through signing up and pledging to do the following:

- Promoting fair play and encouraging others to do the same – I understand we play hockey for fun and this is not the Olympics.
- Accepting the decisions of officials and encouraging others to do the same – I understand officials are human and can make mistakes too.
- Thinking before I speak and keeping my emotions in check and encouraging others to do the same – I understand it is never ok to direct offensive, insulting or abusive language or behaviour at officials.

- Thanking officials and encouraging others to do the same – I understand officials volunteer their time and effort.

(Hockey NSW, 2020)

As of early 2020 the "take the pledge" campaign had received over 2,000
pledges, with the campaign receiving support from Hockey Australia at the
Under 21 Field Nationals in Sydney. The umpires wore branded uniforms
and the campaign was promoted through Hockey Australia's social media
channels and signage at the Sydney Olympic Park Hockey Centre. A poster
was also created by Hockey NSW to promote the "take the pledge" campaign (see Figure 7.1).

Improving the situation: promoting a positive way forward

Throughout this book we have considered how abuse impacts upon match
officials in sport. The nature of this abuse has been considered, as has the
support network which exists around match officials and the challenges a
reduced support system can present. We have considered how these issues
extend beyond and across national and international boundaries, evidencing
the concerted and growing trends which transcend traditional geographi-
cal boundaries (see Chapter 6). Nevertheless, this chapter has focused on
examples of good practice and innovation as a means of advancing the conversation regarding the abuse and support of match officials. As such it is
also important to focus on improving the situation and investigating potential policy implications and methods to improve the existing state of affairs.
Whilst these initiatives are admirable, and the organisations devising and
delivering them are seeking to address the extent of abuse match officials
are exposed to through awareness campaigns and supportive mechanisms,
much of this provision is disjointed within and across sports. We have,
therefore, created a 10-point plan to control and reduce abuse, increase support and improve retention (see Table 7.1).

This 10-point plan is designed to address the concerns raised and explored
in this book and begin to promote and move towards a joined-up approach to
addressing some of the biggest and most complex issues raised throughout
the analysis of the data. The plan outlined next involves a series of targeted
and structured methods which will assist the required increased recruitment
of potential match officials, alongside improved retention of current match
officials. Aspects of the plan can operate independently or in unison for further impact. The plan is developed as an extension of the conceptual model
of the factors influencing match official welfare and future outcomes, presented in Chapter 5 (see Figure 5.1), which identified the current personal,
environmental and societal factors impacting upon match officials, as well

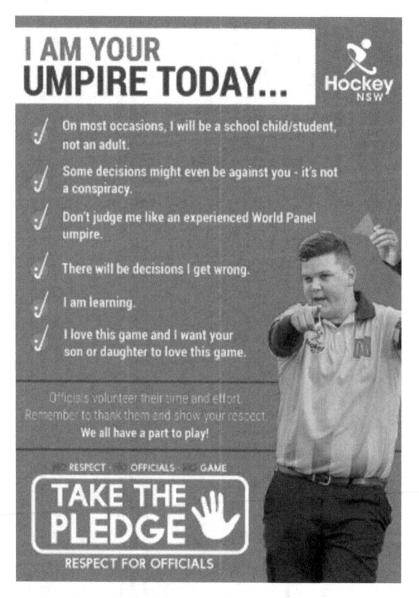

Figure 7.1 Take the pledge campaign poster
Source: (Adapted from Hockey NSW).

Table 7.1 10-point plan to control and reduce abuse, increase support and improve retention

Key Points	Explanation	Further Context	Future Outcomes
1 Sharing, disseminating and implementing policy change	Sports to begin structured, targeted dialogue to learn from best practice and initiatives and policy changes which have been unsuccessful.	**Local/regional level** – To be introduced within countries, beginning with regional networks, sharing information through meetings across sports. **National level** – Alongside this, governing bodies in each country should begin formalised, timely meetings and workshops. Focusing on policy sharing and collaborative approaches, tackling some of the issues identified below and also identifying concerns as they develop. **International level** – This will increase and develop the collaborative approach at the highest level of governance.	**Increased collaboration** – this will result in shared approaches and increased success from these approaches as best practice is understood, as well as initiatives that have not been successful. **Increased numbers of match officials in sport** – more match officials recruited and retained within sports due to the increased knowledge across sports.
2 Supporting and developing young match officials	Identify and support underage match officials. This should begin from the initial course and continue up to **two years** into their officiating journey, with evidence suggesting that match officials are most likely to leave within two years of their initial course.	Provide observers and mentors for young match officials. Observers can record any issues/problems with players, spectators and coaches that referees might miss, and provide further professional development points. Mentors can also provide development, as well as increased support. It is recognised that there is a personnel issue in terms of numbers, but the benefits outweigh the challenges.	**Increased support networks for young match officials** – improved support and training, leading to continuous professional development (CPD) and potential development tools will, in turn, provide a more inclusive environment for young match officials. This will lead to improved retention.

| 3 Reinvigorate the disciplinary procedures | The same issues with disciplinary systems occur across sports and countries. Disciplinary systems are flawed: there is a lack of support for match officials within the process, a lack of communication and issues related to young match officials, as well as a duty of care. | Linked to the requirement for improved support systems. Match officials feel unsupported when involved in the disciplinary process, leading to cultures of non-reporting of incidents. | **Improved knowledge for governing bodies** – currently National Governing Bodies (NGBs) at national and international level do not know the full extent of the issues due to non-reporting. **Improved support for match officials** – also increasing their faith in the systems. |
| 4 Increased support through helplines | Sports to provide helplines for match officials. This can be to support them after abusive situations and to provide ongoing support as is required in each individual case. | Match officials across sports have stated that the support systems around them are not considered adequate enough. | **Improved support for match officials** – fewer match officials discontinuing following abuse-related incidents. **Improved information for disciplinary procedures** – match officials can be guided through the requisite procedures by the phoneline operator. This will lead to improved disciplinary processes. |

(Continued)

Table 7.1 (Continued)

Key Points	Explanation	Further Context	Future Outcomes
5 Increased visibility and information regarding mental health and wellbeing	Mental health and wellbeing support for match officials. This should be introduced as compulsory for governing bodies and match official organisations throughout the season. It is especially important following an abusive incident.	Governing bodies and match official support organisations to consider the construction of initiatives/programmes that provide mental health and wellbeing support for their match officials. Information sharing on this subject between sports should be encouraged.	**Increased educational information for match officials** – this information should address incidents of abuse, coping with incidents of abuse, the importance of good mental health and wellbeing and reducing feelings of isolation.
6 Campaigns promoting the importance of match officials	Dedicated and concerted campaigns to increase understanding about the role of match officials and the challenges they face. Match officials are often an essential aspect of the majority of sports and therefore players, coaches and spectators should understand the impact of decreasing numbers of match officials.	Governing bodies and leagues to consider how clubs could receive incentives/benefits for signing up and adhering to promotional campaigns. Evidence can be demonstrated through club initiatives across age groups, evidence in competitive matches and inclusive schemes aimed at match officials themselves. Status could be assisted by increasing/ introducing fees payable, as well as increased support systems around match officials.	**Short/Medium term** – the improved status of match officials within the sport in question would be assisted by increasing/introducing fees payable to match officials. This would help to further incentivise development skills and competencies of the workforce and increase support systems around match officials. **Long term** – elevate the status of match officials. This will come from some of the actions from clubs and leagues, but also from the messages from governing bodies and the subsequent actions.

| 7 **Microphones on match officials** | Mostly related to the elite game. The introduction of microphones on all match officials would assist in improving player behaviour. This would particularly apply to football. | Increased player behaviour in the elite game would also impact upon player, coach and spectator behaviour at lower levels. Match officials believed that there is a clear link. | **Elite game** – the introduction of microphones would improve player and coach behaviour towards match officials. Particularly if transgressions were strongly discouraged by leagues and governing bodies. **Youth and grassroots game** – behaviour would improve as actions in the professional game were enhanced, leading to fewer abusive/confrontational incidents, and reduced discontinuation. |
| 8 **Whole game approaches** | Unified whole game approaches. Initiatives proposed in this plan require buy-in from all stakeholders, otherwise if any such campaign or programme does not permeate the whole game, it is far more difficult for any initiative to operate effectively. | Match officials discussed requirements for the lead to be taken from the professional games. Without the exposure and coverage from the professional games, the message of any initiative will be limited. Further impact could be achieved by sports operating together, sharing resources and implementing shared campaigns. This would achieve greater impressions. The top players and coaches have to show in their actions how to behave. This will, in time, affect sport at lower levels. | **Increased impact** – impact would increase from any initiatives with the inclusion of the professional leagues. **Change in culture** – cultural change takes time, but it has to be initiated by the entire sport. Increasing the recruitment and retention of match officials would be far easier if the environment in which many of them operate was more inviting. |

(Continued)

Table 7.1 (Continued)

Key Points	Explanation	Further Context	Future Outcomes
9 Resolve conflict between stakeholder groups	Conflict resolution training and workshops for match officials. Conflict resolution workshops for match officials, players, coaches and spectators.	Reducing the isolation of match officials is imperative. This isolation begins at grassroots level and can lead to match officials leaving their chosen sport. Dealing with the issues match officials face as a group is important, despite the need to improve the environment in which match officials operate. It is also important to address the apparent disconnect between match officials, players, coaches and spectators within sport in order to improve the situation.	**Dealing effectively with abuse and conflict** – the introduction of conflict resolution for match officials will decrease the number of abusive events. It will also enable match officials to deal with these situations more appropriately when they do arise. **Change in culture** – understanding of the role of the match official, and improving communication between match officials, players, coaches and spectators will improve the culture around the sport in question.
10 The importance of future research	Future research development is required to increase our understanding around the role and demands of officiating.	Areas of research such as mental health, cultural differences between sports and countries and why players, coaches and spectators behave negatively towards match officials are all important areas to focus upon and have gaps in understanding. This research should be focused on specific sports, comparing sports and also across countries to evidence any wider trends that those in positions of governance should be aware.	**Increased research output** – increased research will help governing bodies of sport to arrest any declines in match official populations and to increase support for match officials. **Increased links between academics and the sport sector** – increased research and engagement by academics will initiate further links with those operating with match officials in sport. The increased research output can assist in developing a progressive environment around match officials.

as the potential outcomes should some of these factors remain unaddressed. Therefore, the plan attempts to deal with the issues raised in the conceptual model, and provide solutions to the identified challenges, including the role of future research related to sports match officials.

This plan and the initiatives therein will take time to implement and for any associated results to become observable. Reducing abuse will involve cultural change (Webb, 2017), and the focus should continue to be on dealing with the consequences of any abuse, whilst also impacting positively on the retention of match officials. For example, research understanding mental health and wellbeing is particularly important, especially for those match officials who are subjected to various forms of abuse (see for example Chapter 5). There are examples of sporting organisations beginning to consider the importance of good mental health and wellbeing for match officials (The FA, 2019b, 2020), although this is in its infancy. We are still unaware of the effect of an abusive incident upon any match official's mental health and wellbeing, with further research in this area required to enhance a better understanding (Gorczynski & Webb, 2020; Webb & Gorczynski, in press).

There are some aspects of the 10-point plan which can be instigated more quickly and therefore can make fairly rapid enhancements to the experiences of match officials, and the wider environment in which match officials operate. For example, point 1 (sharing, disseminating and implementing policy change) can be initiated by governing bodies in different sports and the preliminary processes can be employed relatively quickly. The outcomes from these meetings, the shared understanding which these meetings can generate and the subsequent policy change take longer to be implemented and accepted by the governing bodies and the match officials themselves. Moreover, point 4 (increased support through helplines) has similar characteristics. The helpline can be set up relatively quickly, but the training for those on that helpline, potentially dealing with verbal and physical abuse amongst other issues, takes longer to arrange and deliver. Staffing the helpline altogether is a considerable undertaking.

Finally, point 7 (microphones on match officials) can also be initiated quickly, with the acceptance of governing bodies, leagues and organisations such as UEFA and FIFA in football, depending on the competition in question. Nevertheless, the introduction of microphones onto match officials is the first step, but the extent to which the microphones will change the behaviour of players and coaches will take longer to comprehend. This will involve altering the actions of players and coaches, which have been in existence for potentially as long as they have played their sport, and this level of behavioural change is not a quick process.

Overall, this book has investigated in extensive detail the experiences of match officials across sports and countries, and the result of the analysis of the data has led to the construction of this 10-point plan. It is considered that the implementation of this plan, or elements of it, will lead to increased support of match officials, improved recruitment and increased retention, all of which are ongoing concerning matters in sport, particularly when linked to the verbal and physical abuse evident across this book.

Conclusion

We can see from the coverage of the interventions and examples of good practice in this chapter that there is some innovative and positive work taking place. Sports governing bodies and wider organisations have shown that there is an understanding of the importance of the role of match officials within their sports, and some of the initiatives explored in this chapter have clearly sought to increase understanding and support for these match officials. However, these interventions are not widespread, and in many sports there are concerns regarding the support that match officials receive. It is understood that some sports have greater financial resources than others and are therefore better placed to be able to instigate change. Nevertheless, this book has sought to identify interventions that cover a range of matters, some of which would be a greater financial commitment, others which would not be financially prohibitive.

The examples from England involved initiatives such as the yellow armband designed to support young referees by alerting players, coaches and spectators that the referee is young, and therefore requires some additional understanding, due to their developing experience and potential vulnerability. In the Netherlands the KNVB has partnered with organisations such as 24/7 and Halt to provide increased support for their referees. This support has involved the creation of a phoneline for referees which amongst other things deals with physical threats or confrontation with physical injury due to violence or aggression and an impaired physical or mental condition as a result of violence or aggression. Furthermore, Halt aims to combat juvenile delinquency and targets youth football players who are given bans over violent attacks, with these young players offered behavioural training, with attendance incentivised through the potential reduction of suspensions (KNVB, n.d.b).

The examples in Australia included the "take the pledge" initiative introduced by Hockey New South Wales. The campaign encouraged players, teams, spectators and clubs to champion the respect of umpires through taking the pledge. The pledge included, amongst other things, accepting the decisions of the match officials and encouraging others to do the same and understanding that it is never acceptable to direct offensive, insulting or abusive language or behaviour at officials (Hockey NSW, 2020).

As we have discovered in this book, the abuse of match officials is not an issue for one country or one sport, it is a growing concern across the world. How we deal with this issue requires careful consideration because the abuse of match officials has been evident for generations, and yet the problem persists. However, the apparent reduction in the numbers of match officials, through reduced recruitment and retention, leaves many sports at a crossroads. Implementing change, such as that outlined in the 10-point plan, can take time, and time is a commodity that many governing bodies do not have when it comes to the declining numbers of match officials. Joined up and collaborative approaches between sports, who often share trends related to match official abuse and support, is a starting point and should be encouraged. One choice that is not acceptable is to do nothing. We are considerably past that juncture.

References

Cleland, J., O'Gorman, J., & Bond, M. (2015). The English football association's respect campaign: The referees' view. *International Journal of Sport, Policy and Politics*, *7*(4), 551–563. doi: 10.1080/19406940.2015.1088050

Cleland, J., O'Gorman, J., & Webb, T. (2018). Respect? An investigation into the experience of referees in association football. *International Review for the Sociology of Sport*, *53*(8), 960–974. doi: 10.1177/1012690216687979

The FA. (2019a). *As "sin bins" are introduced to grassroots football, find out how it might affect you.* Retrieved from www.thefa.com/news/2019/jul/29/sin-bins-launched-for-2019-20-season-290719

The FA. (2019b). *Mental health, spotting the signs, supporting, signposting: For coaches and managers in adult football clubs.* Retrieved from www.thefa.com/about-football-association/heads-up

The FA. (2020). *The FA mental health guidance notes for referees.* Retrieved from www.thefa.com/news/2020/feb/05/referee-mental-health-guidance-notes-lucy-briggs-account-060220

Gorczynski, P. & Webb, T. (2020). Call to action: The need for a mental health research agenda for sports match officials. Managing Sport and Leisure. doi: 10.1080/237540472.2020.1792803

Hockey ACT Umpire Handbook. (2013). Retrieved from https://hockeyact.org.au/wp-content/uploads/2019/10/2013-HACT-umpire-handbook.pdf

Hockey NSW. (2020). *Take the pledge: Respect for officials.* Retrieved from www.hockeynsw.com.au/latest-news/respect-for-officials-pledge/

KNVB. (n.d.a). *Noodnummer en nazorg bij geweld op het veld.* Retrieved from www.knvb.nl/assist/assist-scheidsrechters/wedstrijdinformatie/noodnummer-en-nazorg

KNVB. (n.d.b). *Aanpak halt en knvb.* Retrieved from www.knvb.nl/assist/assist-bestuurders/verenigingsbeleid/sportiviteit-en-respect/aanpak-halt-en-knvb

Rathborn, J. (2019). *FA introduce 10-minute sin bins across grassroots football in bid to tackle dissent.* Retrieved from www.independent.co.uk/sport/football/

premier-league/the-fa-sin-bins-grassroots-football-dissent-referees-2019-20-season-a9026601.html

RefSupport. (n.d.). *RefSupport advice hotline*. Retrieved from https://refsupport.co.uk

Ridinger, L. L., Kim, K. R., Warner, S., & Tingle, J. K. (2017a). Development of the referee retention scale. *Journal of Sport Management, 31*(5), 514–527. doi: 10.1123/jsm.2017-0065

Ridinger, L. L., Warner, S., Tingle, J. K., & Kim, K. R. (2017b). Why referees stay in the game. *Global Sport Business Journal, 5*(3), 22–37.

Webb, T. (2017). *Elite soccer referees: Officiating in the Premier League, La Liga and Serie A*. London: Routledge.

Webb, T., Cleland, J., & O'Gorman, J. (2017). The distribution of power through a media campaign: The respect programme, referees and violence in association football. *The Journal of Global Sport Management, 2*(3), 162–181. doi: 10.1080/24704067.2017.1350591

Webb, T., & Gorczynski, P. (in press). Factors influencing the mental health of sports match officials: The potential impact of abuse and a destabilised support system from a global context. In M. Lang (Ed.), *The international handbook of athlete welfare*. London: Routledge.

Index

Page numbers in *italic* indicate a figure and page numbers in **bold** indicate a table on the corresponding page.

Printed in the United States
by Baker & Taylor Publisher Services